Toilets

by
Brian Accetta

Copyright ©2008 by Brian Accetta
publisher * nowarman
editor * Donnie "Six" Furlongs
illustration * Kati Pelkey-Simon
ISBN: 978-0-615-26194-2

Foreword

When you open your heart to people and let the skeletons out you find no one escapes. We all feel the pain, the powerlessness, and the selfish thoughts we don't say out loud of a loved one carrying the burden (the monkey). You try to reason, to rationalize, to give comfort. You try to fix blame. You try to find the button to push to turn the "Holy Shit" light on to make sense of it all. Then suddenly it just happens- sometimes good, sometimes bad. (Hello brother Tim. If I ever get a boat it's got your name on it.)

Here's a success story, at least for this day John Bolen. The stories I'm told are true. Hold on to those of you who never faced the toilet tank. Enjoy to those of you that sat both ways. And congratulations to you who thought the top of the toilet tank was a porcelain coke tray and are here to read this.

Catfish, seeing you always makes me smile.

Love Dad. (Ray Accetta)

For Charles Bukowski

I. <u>The Sungroove Liberation Revolution Evolution</u>

I will start by stating that this will be a true account of the times and lives of many people encountered throughout my days of drugs and alcohol filled experiences with the band and other stops I've made along the long road of destruction. No names will be changed, thus no protection for the guilty, especially for me, Eddie Keebler. Only the facts as I recall them, cloudy as they are, will flow from this pen.

The Sungroove Liberation Revolution was born of three wounded veterans of the nineties' revival of rock-n-roll, drugs, and an array of sexual escapades like those told to me from many flower kids of the sixties. Each of us, Beau, Buck, and I had undoubtedly driven many miles along the Underground Railroad scene long before we met. I say this without any hesitation: the three of us were destined to form a band and the events during our brief career unfolded exactly the way they were supposed to. We played every show we had in us, right up to the final one. It was apparent to each of us that we were finished when we stumbled out of The Clam Hut in Long Branch New Jersey sometime in 2005. With Buck on drums, Beau on guitar, and me on bass, we managed to play almost two hundred shows and wrote fifty original songs, of which I believe all were unique. A few miscellaneous people also performed with us providing the band a means of exploring many different styles and genres.

The most aggravating question we'd be asked is "What style of music do you play?" Towards the end I felt like gutting most who asked. People characterized us in many ways: a jam band, psychedelic, shoe gazers, classic rock, alternative, good old fashioned rock-n-roll. I would say we probably were a combination of all of these and many others. One thing for certain, we played and wrote whatever felt good. To some extent I felt like we would have fit in better in the late sixties, early seventies. We certainly would have been more accepted then due to what I feel has been an inevitable decline in the public's ability to appreciate and comprehend good music. It's not their fault though. I blame the industry itself for straying away from the album concept, while pushing people toward empty lyrics with music sounding as if played by children. Fucking terrible actually. It's amazingly shitty to realize this fact but there are things to be done about it. Figure it out for yourself please, as I know what my part is in the whole damn deal.

I remember being totally amazed with music from the very start, even though looking back now and realizing the first slice of music I ever owned was a "Blondie" record my mother bought me when I was six years old. My father got me a record player and big fat headphones and I would turn up the damn volume to the point where my ear drums began their long haul of deterioration and sing like a maniac until someone, my brother, father, or any random house guest burst into my room and tell me to shut the fuck up, and, as much as it pains me to say it, a Barry Manilow eight track would howl from my mother's old Buick with me cackling like a bird singing along. Shit, how grateful I am those days are over.

After brief, I mean brief excursions into the rap scene during my first two years of high school I finally graduated to the good stuff: Beatles, Doors, Floyd, Dylan, HENDRIX, and most of the rest of the classic cats. In my car at one point were solely the sixteen Beatles albums, with the second side of "Abbey Road" serving as my mantra. Sounds of McCartney's bass are etched into their own separate side of my mind forever, to the point of if someone bad mouthed him, and some did, I'd erupt in a rage and smack the shit of them, usually resulting in them apologizing due to the fact that I was the man with the weed. Never bite of the hand that feeds right? That's right.

Buck and I met in grade school and had a scattered friendship with intervals sometimes lasting years. He would always turn me on to some real good tunes, "Swervedriver" and "Ride" come to mind, and I give him all the credit for familiarizing me with the underground scene of the nineties.

We hung out in stages seeming to always renew our friendship as we both progressed through the ladder of drugs. We went into business together distributing the town-famous "Drama Weed" in 1994 which was introduced to us by a cat named Nick who we worked with at a gas station. This weed instantly became the toast of the town and we had a virtual monopoly on the market for a solid year until finally we were burned out from the hassles.

One night while working with Nick it was pouring down rain and he and I sat on a bench under the canopy and fired up a fatty he twisted up and slugged down beers left in the fridge by the owners of the joint. "Can you get rid of some of this shit man?" he asked, after a ten second lull of silence when I realized how good the shit was.

"Yeah man." I quickly responded.

I followed him back to his house after work and he led me into the basement after introducing me to his beautiful wife. After sucking down another joint he told me to open the fridge and take whatever I could handle. The fridge was filled with weed from top to bottom, packed in tight like a virgin's prize.

"You got a duffle bag man, a big one?" I excitedly requested.

I filled it up snug with two pounds of Mother Nature's finest and headed upstairs and out the front door feeling like I just made the score of the century, because I had. He fronted it all to me giving me a week to give him his desired price, which was more than fair. I made a stealth run to Buck's place and dumped the sack on the floor of his room and we got *stoned* as we broke down the chunk into various weighted bags getting ready to hit the streets with the shit.

The best part of having the market cornered was that everyone needed to come through us, which reintroduced me to many of the douche bags I went to high school with. We met my brother's friend Teddy one night and as he leaned against the window of Buck's car I spotted Scott, the quarterback of our team in high school set back on the grass trying to be discreet, the golden boy you dig?

"Hey buddy." I said condescendingly, "you better hold on tight man, this shit's gonna knock you on your ass!"

He looked anything like the superhero jock he was in high school, with the look of a man freaking out on LSD pasted on his face. I loved it. I enjoyed being that kind of guy; the one who people who didn't know me couldn't stand, but needed me to get their fix. Damn fools.

After a while though, the strain of selling pot took its toll on us. We never seemed to have enough time to enjoy the shit ourselves. We'd go to Nick's and break down the stuff then immediately start making deliveries which was a service we provided justifying our high prices. No peace. The whole deal got cut short by the grace of god when the police raided Nick's house thirty minutes before we got there one night.

We passed bye as he was being taken away by Bricktown's finest as his wife and baby girl watched him being taken away in handcuffs, the poor bastard. I did feel like shit about the whole thing for a while, not enough to lose any sleep or anything, just in a man that sucks kind of way.

After he went to prison, for three years, I would stop by to see his wife twice a week to make sure she was okay. Often she was not, crying, strung out on heroin until finally the state took her daughter away one day and rightfully so. I wonder what happened to them sometimes and to their daughter. Oh well.

I also recall a week's worth of mescaline which was thrown to us by a girl just riding through town that same year. She rolled up with a backpack full of beautiful tiny blue microdots instantly becoming a celebrity amongst us. Apparently she followed the Dead and shacked up with the first people she felt a connection with paying them off for room and board with sex, good sex, and trips until it was time for her to move on, a true hippy chick indeed.

I believe during this time Buck and I really got to understand each other while also discovering we were different in our own way. I'm quite sure we would have grown close eventually but trippin out with someone speeds the process tremendously.

I was reunited by Buck by chance in 2000. I unknowingly began dating his cousin, a train wreck of a girl named Heather. She and I were a fucking disaster together, largely because of my rampant drug abuse and drunkenness and her Irish blooded belligerence.

She invited me to her Aunt's house for a barbeque and as we drove there I realized it was Buck's childhood home we were going to. Man I was happy to see Buck's family as we walked in the front door. They were my surrogate parents for a while during Buck's and my sporadic relationship. Their house was a safe haven where no matter how fucked up we all were we could go to it without any initial grueling lectures from his parents until the next day. They didn't like us getting twisted all the time but they understood we were going to anyhow and kind of took comfort when we were there, knowing at least we were alive and relatively safe.

Over whiskey and beers Buck and I sat and bullshitted about everything. I told him about my newly discovered bass playing and he shot back news of his recently acquired talent on the drums. We quickly planned a jam session for the next weekend at his and his wife's house. It just felt right the way the whole thing worked out you know? Smooth like the head of Telly Savalas. Heather and I split up later that day citing an irreconcilable hatred for each other. She was a sweet kid.

Every week for six months Buck and I met at his place and tore it up for a couple of hours in his garage, weaving together his flare for the newer music and mine encompassing the good old shit. We'd write several new songs each week, containing a plethora of changes and speed variations which blow my goddamn mind still. The great thing about just jamming with bass and drums is the bond that's formed not only personally but musically is unshakeable.

The time came when we felt we had plenty of material to reach out and bring in a guitar/singer to complete the band. This person needed to be polished as far as adaptability and freelancing went, a requirement many people we knew certainly did not posses.

Through a friend we learned of some cat named Beau, who was extremely talented on guitar but known on the street as one crazy mother-fucker. At that time, crazy mother-fuckers were just my game, so we set up a sort-of tryout on a Tuesday evening.

Regarding Beau: we gave him many nicknames through the years; I will try my best to call him Beau, but may refer to him as: the Colonel, Colonel Van Bostrand, Bozwell, Van Beau (I dubbed him that because he couldn't hear for shit so I told him I was going to cut off his ear like Van Gogh and scream into it so he could hear me), Thurston Von Beauregard, Bojangles, Duke of Bearl, and many others which escape me right now.

Roughly two years after we met him, we learned his real name was Nicholas Yerks. He was excited to learn that his estranged father was sending him three thousand dollars. He assured Buck and I he'd spend it on vital equipment needed for playing out. His father made the check out to "Beau". As this was just a nickname, the bank naturally refused to cash it, rightfully so. I remember Beau telling us his conversation with the bank teller: "Are you trying to say I'm not Beau? Don't I *look* like a Beau?" to no avail he argued. I'm not sure whatever happened as far as a new check, but I can tell you we didn't get new equipment.

The thing was he did look like a Beau. He was exactly the person mothers told their little girls to stay away from. He dressed in retro vintage clothes purchased only at thrift shops. It was as if they were tailored exclusively for him.

His sideburns were a cross between Elvis and John Lennon and I assure you, they took a backseat to neither. I recall one day when he and I met for drinks with Adolf Hitler mustaches. I brought a razor in case I pussed out, but he convinced me not to.

And the word on the street was correct. He was a crazy son-of-a-bitch. He reminded me mostly of Jim Morrison in that when anyone offered us drugs, he always took them on the spot. He had no regard for what else he had to do that day. He was purely a moment-by-moment creature and I can say without any chance of untruth that he *never* said "No"- to drugs or booze.

I finally found someone who partied and thought as I did. Looking back, it was definitely one of the most significant days of my life when I met him. We endured many chaotic times, countless close calls, and our fair share of visits with New Jersey's finest. Truth be told, we both belong in prison for life along with Buck serving ten to twenty. Instead we're all free and I'm reliving it all writing this goddamn book. Sounds fair to me.

So far as Beau's guitar playing I can't begin to convey how heavy his style was. First of all, he's a lefty who plays a right-handed guitar upside down like Hendrix, but unlike Hendrix he didn't have it re-strung the correct way. He couldn't afford a guitar, let alone a left-handed one as a kid, so he learned by playing his friend's right-handers upside down. As he matured in his playing, he decided to keep it that way rather than to switch to a natural left handed guitar. Needless to say, but I'll say it anyway; he was self taught and in fact plays exactly the opposite way of any other guitarist. Lessons were out of the question for him because no one teaches guitar ass-backwards. It was apparent to me early on that he wouldn't have taken them anyway. He didn't need to. It was all feel for him, as it was for all of us. Straight from the soul, no sugar coat. I was always blown away when people finally realized he was playing all this incredible shit with an upside down guitar like a maniac, as they would come up to us after shows to elaborate on just how much their minds had been fucked by the sound ringing throughout the night. His style alone got us all laid more than a couple of times. We played with an all chick band once that were, let's say very *impressed*, as were we.

So on that fateful Tuesday evening Buck and I were jamming in his garage as a car drove up, parked halfway on the lawn, and out fell Beau literally.

I'm not sure exactly what kind of wheels he had, but I recall it being long, old, and dark. After knowing him for a while, maybe three hours, the car most definitely reflected his personality. Roughly a week later he bought a new car, some cheap compact of sorts. He drove it for seven days then crashed in Seaside, New Jersey. Apparently he was high on pills and booze when he came to a point when he could go left or right. He decided to go straight. Consequently he lost his license, totaled his car, and has never driven to this 22nd day of October 2007. He was eligible to renew his license in 2002.

We helped the Colonel with his guitars and amp then got set up in the garage. Without hesitation, he plugged in and immediately began howling on his guitar. I was floored. We played two hours with minimal breaks for cigarettes. He had a groove for everything Buck and I had been putting together. Upon finishing, he asked so matter-of-factly, "Well, am I in the band?"

I said, "Brother, you *are* the band."

We found out the next day Beau was ripped up on heroin for the jam. We jammed one of his songs, "Warm Breeze Baby" at the end of our first session the previous day. After he told us he was strung out the day before, he remarked so lavishly, "Hey, that song's not about a chick man."

For the next few days we all hung out together day and night, jamming, boozing, snorting, and smoking whatever we got our hands on. Buck and I quickly got a sense of how off the wall Beau was when he grabbed a unsuspecting patron at a bar we closed each night by the throat and tossed him to the ground only because he though the cat was wearing a better looking fat collared shirt than he was, as Beau was the king of the vintage scene you see.

Earlier that afternoon Beau threw a beer at another dude in the bar we ate breakfast at because the man was sitting in his seat, the seat Beau sat on for two days straight so naturally it was *his*. How he fit in with us though, completing the trio like peanut butter, jelly, and bread: fucking tasty!

I took more of an immediate liking to Beau than Buck because he got just as tore up as I did. Up until meeting him I was the incumbent loose canon anywhere I went. Evidently Beau wore out his welcome with just about everyone he knew from being the bad egg, the demon child, as not once did he receive or make a call during our five day binge together. Even the worst of folk hear from someone sometimes no?

Brothers to the bone he and I turned out to be. Our conversations revealed ourselves to each other not by words, but by tone, body language and looks in our eyes and faces which spoke far louder. The same went for jamming. We knew from the get go how to compliment each other, and with Buck pounding the drums man it was thick. I mean of course I am heavily biased but our sound was one of which I'd never heard before.

A week later we had the privilege to see Adam Franklin of "Swervedriver" perform a solo acoustic set at "The Sinner" in lovely Asbury Park, New Jersey. Buck, Beau, and I picked up this married chick named Jocelyn, who I assure you was neither happily married nor faithful as Buck had been filling her with his juice for a few months. Beau was whacked out on heroin, pills, and booze, and brought a sack of blow with him that we all enjoyed on the ride up and throughout the evening. It's hilarious that he was the one who brought the coke. It was the only time since I've known him that he was the guy who had it. I guess he figured he better make it seem like he was able to contribute in some way, a sort of initiation where once he was fully sworn into our group he could just ride our coat tails into oblivion. And hell did he.

Adam Franklin had such an eloquent sound that night, took many requests, and nailed them all. About halfway through the show the Colonel approached Scott, the owner/operator of "The Sinner". He told him of his new band and that we would be looking for shows in the coming months. Beau's previous band played many shows there. Scott replied, "What are you guys doing Tuesday? I need an opening act."

Without consulting us Beau booked the show, and when asked what the name of our band was he replied with the first thought that entered his clouded mind: The Sungroove Liberation Revolution.

We all drove home in my car that night full of hope, joy, whiskey, wine, pills, and blow, floating on a cloud the whole way. Fuck yeah we'll play on Tuesday.

We made that place shiver in awe that Tuesday night. Rock n' roll chicks all drunk and ready to go. Cocaine by the bucket full and intravenous booze set on a quick drip, yeah, I could dig being a musician. That would work. We played a short thirty minute sat and left the place wanting more. We were officially now a band, and a damn good one I must say.

II. <u>The Pussycat</u>

There is absolutely nothing in the world that I've experienced that has come close to jamming in New York City. Everything that I could possibly imagine was laid out before me, ready to be taken. It's like an adult amusement park that never closes, with rides lasting far longer than a virgin to the scene could comprehend. Twenty dollar grams of coke, sacks of weed resembling the one of Santa Claus early on Christmas morning, three dollar whores whose actions made them seem worth much more. I've been in love with the city since day one.

As a band we had been doing well along the Jersey Shore and through another band we were able to book a show at "The Pussycat" in Manhattan.

I received a phone call from the promoter, Billy the Hat. After discussing random events for what seemed like quite a while, we agreed to play there on a Friday night with our set beginning around midnight.

We played a show once with a band called EFPTOZ. Repeat this name a few times. Spell it out. E-F-P-T-O-Z. Get it? Don't feel shitty about it because we didn't either. It's the letters on the chart that you read from top to bottom when you have your eyes examined.

Apparently after this particular show we exchanged phone numbers with these cats, while they spoke about hooking us up with gigs in New York where they played. I don't recall the exact conversation, as many bands we played with had spouted this bullshit on us too many times before so I wasn't very enthused at the time. Spoonfuls of cocaine and bottomless bourbon were surely not helpful factors to my recollections of the evening I'm sure. However, as promised, they delivered us to Billy the Hat.

On the day of the show I took off from work, as usually was the case. I mean we had to be in Manhattan for midnight, a two hour drive, so how the hell could I be expected to work at all let alone until five in the afternoon? Buck was a good boy when it came to work. He went in at nine and stayed until five. Sucker. Beau needed a day off before and after each show, so I picked him up at ten in the morning and we proceeded to the liquor store for a few bottles of breakfast. After washing down some pain killers we began our trek of scoring enough coke to sustain us for the long day ahead.

It's quite comical recalling this day because we could have bought all the coke in town and it wouldn't have been enough. Hell, there was *never* enough.

Beau and I decided to call Buck at one o'clock to persuade him to skip out on work. We explained to him that we were picking up some blow at two o'clock, so it was naturally sensible for him to come join us for the beginning of the snow-filled slopes that we'd be skiing all day. He didn't agree with our reasoning and ridiculed our request. He also made us promise not to get too fucked up too early advising us to pace ourselves and as he finished those words he laughed. Who's being silly now? I thought.

Don't get me wrong. Buck was by no means a square when it came to snorting blow, drinking booze, and popping pills. I've met up with him several dozen times when he was the guy holding the goods. What I'm saying is that if The Sungroove Liberation Revolution was seventy-five percent out of control, Buck was the remaining twenty-five most of the time.

Beau and I picked up the goods at three in the afternoon. One thing's for certain: the man is always late, and we were always early. The next few hours we spent driving up and down the Garden State Parkway making many stops at random bars at every exit between 82 and 109. Beau was the cut man with the blow as I was driving.

This shit was GOOD. My head was numb and I believe Beau may have smoked a mentholated cigarette at my request. He wasn't a smoker but apparently my description of the "Vapor Action" was too thick to pass up.

Holy shit five o'clock! We needed to be at Buck's by six and we were thirty miles from Beau's house where our equipment was. Fuck it. We were lit man. I couldn't even feel my legs and was damn happy about it. We cranked out some "Ride" and enjoyed *everything*. We'd get there eventually. The music echoed throughout my body and at this point I was on auto-pilot. "Chop out two more cannons Beau." He nodded in the affirmative, with a subtle smirk frozen on his face. We were entranced until we arrived at his house.

The Von Beauregard household is the most unique place I have been to up to and including today. His mother was a genuine sweetheart, whose only real concern was that Beau played his guitar and joined a band. She overlooked the drug and alcohol abuse, and after a while we didn't even try to be slick about concealing it.

His grandmother lived there as well. She was old and I'm not sure if she was deaf, a mute, or a combination of the two. What I do know is that they all communicated through a series of claps and other miscellaneous gestures. It wasn't sign language, by no means. Somehow when Beau clapped a few times she knew to give him money. I was tempted to clap myself at times but common decency prevented me.

For some reason I always felt safe there. We would drink, snort coke, smoke weed, and jam out there several times a week. This arrangement was cut short one day when the police arrived. Some of Beau's neighbors, heroin dealers, complained about the noise. As it was only eight p.m. Momma Van Beau refused the officers' request for us to lower the volume, in fact, she pleaded with us to play louder. Shortly thereafter she was arrested and in the back of the police car. I love that woman

Beau's house itself was a hundred years old and not really in the best of shape. The doors were always open and there was no air conditioning in the summer time. We jammed in a tiny room upstairs. In it, were posters you would want hanging up: Hendrix, Morrison, Brianjonestownmassacre, as well as paintings and images from Thurston Von Beauregard himself. Vintage man.

Down the hall were two bedrooms, both belonging to Beau. CD's and scattered drug paraphernalia enveloped the rooms. Stale booze and cigarettes permeated the air. It was perfect.

When we arrived we both ran upstairs to gather our equipment. Still flying from the diesel we snorted, we were in and out of there relatively quickly. We loaded of my Isuzu Rodeo, gave his mother a kiss, and were ready to go to Buck's. Beau clapped his hands and gestured. His grandmother gave him some money.

Not surprisingly Buck was annoyed with us, as we were certainly hammered upon arrival. He quickly got over it when he jammed a rolled up twenty dollar bill up his nose and got himself a taste. At last we were all together, and thus our chaotic night began.

The best thing about the Garden State Parkway is that there are rest areas about every twenty miles, essentially the perfect intervals to stop and chop out a few lines in the bathroom. Doing it in the car gets old quick and my driving at night made it nearly impossible not to lose more than an acceptable amount of cocaine to the deep seats which seemed to devour any morsels that were neglected.

We rolled into the first stop at exit 105 on fire. We owned the night. Laws and common decency did not apply to us. Everything and everyone we came across would undoubtedly take notice to the tornado we stirred and boy, did we love it!

It's a rather large bathroom inside, with two rows of toilets going up and down two hallways. Urinals line the right side with sinks around yet another corner. It's blindingly bright and you could hear the lights themselves breathing amongst the racket of flushes.

At eight o'clock, as it was, it is unbelievable clean and I wouldn't say it smelled pleasantly but I will say that if I absolutely had to take a shit, I would probably feel comfortable enough to do the ole' twelve inches from the bowl hover technique without much fear of what might be splashing me in the ass.

As for the cocaine surface, the back of the toilet, it was clean and smooth, providing an adequate working area for the cut man. On these pit stops, I was usually this guy due to the fact that I couldn't wait for someone else to prepare it. Out of the three of us, I was the fastest with the blade, but definitely the worst. You were always sure to snort a rock of blow along with debris from the toilet when I would cut 'em out. I carved out three ginormous lines, mine being the biggest of course. When it came time to actually snort the line time seemed to slow down, and things got very quiet. I mean there were all kinds of degenerate cocksuckers in there who were traveling along as we were, noisy as fuck and just genuine pricks. When it came time to snort, however, you heard absolutely nothing. The reliable flush and snort came in handy. No one was really fooled by it; they knew what we were doing. It was more a courtesy we would show just to let them know that we knew they knew. Cocaine chivalry if you will.

After indulging myself, I left the twenty and two nice ones in there for Buck and Beau. Beau was next. Another flush. Buck's turn. Down the bowl. A quick piss, a few drinks for the road, and we were off.

After taking another stop at the next rest area for some refreshing, we came upon my favorite stretch of the ride. We hit the Jersey Turnpike and accelerated. You could always go as fast as you wanted on that road, at least we did. I saw people pulled over but never saw cops driving, fortunately.

As we came up to and passed Liberty State Park I felt an overwhelming desire to hear "Radiohead". We saw them play there a couple of years before and it was such a treat. The background of the New York skyline and The Statue of Liberty provided such unbelievable images to go along with their music. Beau found "Hail to the Thief" and I turned it up. It became ritualistic on every return to the city to listen to that disc at that point in the trip.

Ah the Holland Tunnel- the gates of the city- The mouth of the snake. How fitting it is when you take the tunnel into the city. Upon entrance it's like moving indoors while the city streets with her tall buildings protect and provide shelter. Every street looks the same at first, but quickly their uniqueness grabs hold of you, begging you to take their path. It's difficult to say no to them most times.

After a multitude of wrong turns and near accidents we arrived at "The Pussycat" around nine o'clock. We parked right out front on the narrowest of streets and began unloading our equipment. The bouncer at the door informed us to carry our stuff up to the second floor and onto the stage. We learned that we were actually headlining the evening and wouldn't go on until roughly two o'clock.

Since we finished our stash of white gold on the way up, the first order of business was to spot the coke man. Looking back, I believe everyone in there was that "man" in one form another. As we walked up the thin stairway we could hear music bouncing off the walls and although you couldn't smoke indoors in New York anymore many clouds reduced visibility, with colored lights forming kaleidoscoped tunnels from wall to wall.

The first band was due to kick off the night around ten. Many groups of people ranging drastically different filled in the otherwise vast area around the stage and bars. Old men with young chicks. Young chicks with young chicks. Old chicks alone, waiting for the drunken poor bastard to make their way down the ladder to them. How patient they turned out to be.

After a few quick shots and a beer Buck, Beau, and I headed downstairs and outside for a smoke and a conversation with the bouncer. As if he was waiting for us to approach him he initiated the talk by asking. "Whatduya need?"

"Whatduya got?" was our natural response. I love the negotiation part of the drug deal. The end result is invariably the same: a shady deal with us, the consumer, feeling like we got screwed, no matter how good the shit was or how much we got. Something about the action always tickled my balls though. I often wonder what went through the broker's head. Were they nervous, excited, or afraid? When I was that guy I was only thinking about how much I was going to take for myself.

"I've got whatever you need," he said, with an assurance in his voice that made us believe him instantaneously.

"Alright, here's two hundred bucks, we'll take two hundred of the leaded." I said, as if ordering a pound of ham at a deli.

He told us to wait at the door and he'd be right back. We didn't watch where he went, but we knew this brick house of a black man would return quickly, and he didn't disappoint us.

Sweet. A giant rock of blow was hand shook into my grasp, a business like nod was exchanged between him and me, and then Buck, Beau, and I proceeded back inside as if by cannon shot. We burst through the doors of the first floor like Doc Holliday and the Earp boys surely must have back in the day.

Holy shit what a scene on the first floor- A collage of strippers throughout the floor, on stage, and in the dark corners working the night. Tits and ass by the bushel. First things first though- where's the fucking toilet? We'd seek our entertainment afterwards.

In the back of the club was a closet of a bathroom with one stall, one urinal, and light as bright as an interrogation room. With enough room for two, four people waited inside. This would be a challenge but a task of monumental importance laid in wait.

I was first in the stall, deferring the urinal twice in order to enter the work area. Naturally the guy before me took a tremendous shit and judging from the razorblade like smell hitting my nose I can guarantee he spent quite some time in there. I crushed the boulder of coke inside the bag and dumped a sizeable portion onto the back of the toilet, as I didn't want to come back there in five minutes and relive the stank of death too quickly. The surface on which the coke laid was absolutely fucking nasty containing some form of dirt which was probably mixed with all sorts of poisonous elements from all the drugs and miscellaneous debris which a bathroom stall can accumulate. I loved it for being there though, the bathroom that is.

It was so damn humid in the joint that chopping the coke was extremely difficult, damn near impossible. I did my best and cut out three gypsy moth like lines of heaven, then fired one up my nose as I flushed the toilet. With a renewed energy I walked out passing the rolled bill to Beau, then he to Buck, and out to the stripper infested club we returned.

A black man about eight feet tall wearing an exquisitely tailored black suit greeted us with handshakes and a coke filled smile. He was hip to us and likewise so we hit it off immediately. I figured he must have worked there seeing as he more dressed up than anyone else inside. I later learned he was just some cat diggin in on the music, whores, and drugs, a good man indeed.

I told him we were playing later on that night and also that the coke we just bought was outstanding. I offered him a taste but he politely refused, stating he had plenty of his own. He then turned us on to perhaps the most valuable information which would make this night and every return to The Pussycat such a treat- The deli next door sold coke and virtually every other drug imaginable, but of course you had to know how to go about getting it. A sort of password was necessary. You could greet the guy inside with a "hey man" or "what's up?" or any other kind of bullshit, but you had to say it with a certain tone so you understood each other. After that, it was on, I mean you could speak openly about what you needed, the price, and how much. You always bought some regular shit as well just for your own piece of mind. One Twix, one Heineken, that's one hundred my friend.

Anyhow, as it was, we had plenty of coke left from our previous purchase, so we had some fun with the strippers for a while, enjoying their hospitality. We'd surely check out the deli later on.

Like any other strip club there were several ladies who really had no business being naked when others were around, but, of course you gave them courtesy looks and a buck or two just because hell, someone had to.

Buck, Beau, and I passed the blow back and forth for a while, making our own separate trips to the toilet. We began to hear music from upstairs so we smacked a few more asses and proceeded up the catacombed stairwell to pay our respects to the opening band.

And there he was, the Hat. He stood about five foot four and wore his signature black top hat in a way that can only be described as perfect. Thick black glasses covered his bloodshot eyes, while his grayish beard told stories about rough living which he surely must have endured. A vintage black, rusty old suit covered his booze ridden body, with jacket sleeves a bit too short, thus revealing the age of it as well as the torment he put his body through. As I was blinded by his shiny black shoes he began to speak.

"Hey guys I'm Billy. You must be The Sungroove Liberation Revolution. The guys from EFPTOZ told me you cats were alright. How the hell are ya? You need any blow or pussy? How do you set up? How many microphones do you need? Who plays what? I'm gonna get a drink man; see you guys in a bit. And he was gone.

Evidently he did as much coke as we did only he'd been doing it for much longer of course. He looked like he was sixty although forty-something was probably correct. He sounded as if he swallowed a bucket of nails and washed them down with a gallon of scotch every day for the past twenty years or so. He did fit the bill though, and anyone who offered me cocaine and or pussy was a solid citizen of the world in my book.

I don't recall much of the first band, as I was in the groove of checking out the layout of the place. The stage was four feet from the floor and twenty five feet wide at least .As always Buck would play drums in the back of Beau and I, centered of course. With the Colonel being lefty and I right handed, he always took the right side facing the crowd so we wouldn't smack guitars during the show.

The second band hit the stage around midnight, and there was a chick playing the bass, which always turned me on. She was tall, with long straight brown hair down to her ass, which was incredible in its own right. Normally when I see a bass player using a pick I dismiss them for cowards immediately. It's fucking cheating you know, as all soul leaves your fingers when you use it. It's as if it jettisons from the pick and is unable to transfer to the four fat strings which beg for stroking. She, however, was granted a pass due to her unbelievable ass and a smile cut from rainbows.

Buck, Beau, and I finished all the coke we had, so I took advantage of the deli next door. The goddamn batch they sold us was hardly stepped on at all, unveiling an absolute catapult of energy in our bodies after snorting it, allowing us to not only dig on the total scene much harder but also assuring us that we were clearly going to blow the fucking roof off this joint. Man, I can still taste it.

The bathroom in the strip club was even more crowded now so it was impossible to try to hide the whole charade of flushing while snorting. And fuck it; at this point we didn't give a hell anyway. We were on top of the world and about to hit the stage for the first time in New York Fucking City, the Giant Apple, The Tits and The Ass, as I liked to put it. "Better cut yourselves out a few lines boys." I said. , "We've got a long set ahead."

With bellies full of booze and coke-filled egos we hit the stage. We opened with "Beautiful Pharmaceutical", a two and half instrumental that grabbed you by the balls and never let go. The ovation we received after it was like another line of blow straight to my brain, and sustained me for the rest of the set.

Looking out amongst the sardine can like audience I panned from left to right, searching for the inevitable whores who would be waiting for us when we were finished. Many of the strippers had come up to see us as well, assuring us of plenty of action. I mean, as far as "The Pussycat" went, from ground floor to the VIP room we visited afterwards, we were *it*. The headliners, the gods, we were IT.

We closed the set with a ten minute medley of "Rudy" into "Good Fone", a bluesy melodic saga about love, peace, and finding true happiness. The roar came again begging us for an encore, but we refused. We made our mark and left them wanting more, and goddamn it I needed a drink.

After packing up my bass I hurried off the stage in order to shovel some blow up my nose and get that much needed bourbon and beer. A man, much older than anyone else, approached me. He extended his arm and as I extended mine I couldn't help but notice his shaking hand had only two fingers and a thumb. What the fuck? His grip was extra firm, and I thought he'd never let go. This had a nauseating effect on me to say the least.

I don't know about anyone else, but it's my opinion that shaking hands is the most disgusting custom ever introduced into society. I think of myself as a rather tidy individual but I can assure you that if a day in the life of my hands was documented and examined there would surely be all kinds of rancid micro-organisms crawling within, searching for new hosts to infiltrate. I've also found that most people do not wash their hands as frequently as I do, which can only guarantee the cesspool of shit on their hands to be magnified tremendously. I'd love to see a new method of greeting introduced into society. Perhaps we can all bump asses or at least smack each others', Christ!

So the man missing two fingers laid praise on us regarding our performance and invited us up to the VIP floor for a post-show gathering. Of course we accepted, our noses twanging at the thought of what was on the horizon.

There stood a shithouse of a black man at the entrance to the VIP. He must have known we were coming as he congratulated us on a great show and let us in.

The room was dark and empty. Long red couches with black pillows placed perfectly lined the walls. Other than the black cat, we were alone. No one was behind the bar which prompted some anxiety on us all. At this point we decided to hit the bathroom and chop some lines, big ones.

As I headed into the bathroom I noticed the far side of the room actually opened up into a balcony overlooking the stage. The carpet was dark red and begged me to lay on it. Large mirrored tables complimented the couches and tall bar tables and chairs were scattered about the room.

You would think the bathroom would have been a palace, rivaling one of Caligula or at least Pablo Escobar's. It was not. The door didn't lock, which didn't matter at the time for us, but I found it perplexing nonetheless. There was one stall, one urinal, and a sink. The temperature rose twenty degrees as we entered while the already dimly lit room got darker.

Beau went to work on the back of the toilet. I tried to piss, to no avail. It's hard to piss after boozing with blow involved sometimes. Buck was hammered and at a loss for words. The cocaine surface was on an angle, and riddled with scratches from previous chopping episodes. Much debris laid in the cracks.

We did our best, snorting three lines each, and walked back out into the empty room. As we sat on the couch we heard some rumblings coming up the stairway. There was no denying the ten-penny nail voice of Billy the Hat leading the way.

He approached us with a bottle of champagne and following him came thirty girls from the crowd and the strip joint from the first floor, shaking their asses like the cheerleaders from catholic school I remember so well. There were also so random dudes following them, and, I must admit, even thought the ratio of chicks to dicks was roughly six to one, I still was annoyed at their presence for a minute or so.

Billy dropped a baseball sized chunk of blow on the mirrored table and sang us much praise as our music had undoubtedly lit a stick of dynamite up his ass. He immediately booked us for follow up shows at the "Pussycat" as well as other clubs he ran in the city.

There was no need for the toilet as a snorting lounge. Everything was in the open, loud and uninhibited. An orgy of cocaine, booze, and broads, what's better than that? I didn't even mind the random ugly girl over there or there or anywhere. I didn't mind *anything*.

You just haven't lived until you've snorted a line off a chick's ass as she devoured another girl lying beneath her. I love this city. I love Billy the Hat and he loved us. The band was alright.

III. <u>The Clam Hut</u>

As I begin to think of all the shows we played at "The Clam Hut" my nose begins to twitch, while my face becomes numb. Nestled in a corner of Long Branch, New Jersey, three blocks from the beach, this joint began as a large two thousand square foot rock of cocaine. Artisans drenched in rock n' roll cut, chiseled, and carved out a playground for original bands, local and national, to showcase their multitudes of talent. Blessed by the vampires on coke who roamed the Jersey Shore for countless years, these artisans sculpted out a "Helter Skelter" like slide for themselves.

By artisans, I mean Buck, Beau, and I. By the two thousand square foot rock of cocaine I'm referring to a ballpark figure regarding the ridiculous amount we surely had our hands on throughout our shows there.

The "Clam" was home. There were never any rules there right from the start. The stage was our living room, the bartenders and patrons our whores, and Tommy, the man who booked the shows was our buddy. He's without question the coolest cat I've come across in the entire music scene.

Tommy stands five feet six inches from the ground and built like a tank circa de World War II. His grayish brown beard and mustache extended roughly one foot from his face and I assure you that if necessary it could be used to strangle someone, lifting them from the ground until finally all circulation ceased.

With a shaved head and a pair of skull stomping boots Tommy is one of the few I would insist on joining me if things got out of hand and fisticuffs were imminent. Visions of the grand Viking invasions into Europe come to mind when I think of what it would be like to go into battle with this man. I can see blood spewing from people's heads and limbs from repeated battle axe swings, each one precisely measured, certain to kill.

Let's get back to the beard for a moment. I've come across many cats that had beards resembling Tommy's. I've never gotten close enough to any of them to recall a distinct smell, good, or bad. With close proximity necessary for communication, due to loud music and drunken patrons, I was force to get close to Tommy on a nightly basis in order to converse about the evening and what was expected of us when we took the stage. I recall more than a few times when physical contact with his beard occurred and the smell of rotten potatoes still pierces my nostrils to this day. It's as if he used it to wipe the bar down at the end of the night, then cleaned the ashtrays with it. Holy Fuck, I'm choking as I write this! I swear to you I saw some gypsies picking tomatoes from it one night, although it might have been the acid I swallowed which prompted such a vision.

Comprehending the words Tommy spoke was also a chore. His voice had hair on it; his words underwent a full blown pinball game as they came out. It usually took two or three sentences to figure out if he was pissed off at me or not. At that point a few people would walk in and like a vulture he'd run to the door to collect their money.

An L-shaped bar grabs your eye upon entering the jaws of "The Clam". A pool table remains in the middle of the floor until an hour before the first band hits the stage. The stage itself is immediately on the right, three feet from the floor. A platform for the drums was centered onstage up against the back wall, with fifteen feet of room on each side of it for the rest of the band.

Continuing down the right side of the place a wall of black bricks with the names of now sort of famous bands written on them provided a bit class to an otherwise hole in the earth kind of place. A twenty by twenty foot room lined the back right corner, which inside was a place where bands could hang out and get ready for their set, although most bands didn't bother hanging out in there. Only the genuine douche bags would stay in there, waiting to make some sort of grand entrance, only to find themselves showered with chants of "Assholes" as they came out.

A sound room fills out the back of the club, off the floor a few feet. A multitude of mixing boards and recording equipment left only enough room for the engineer inside, although, on many occasions I would chop out some coke for he and I, depending on who was manning it for the night.

There's a door which leads to a parking lot out back just past the toilets. Ah, the toilets. One for chicks, one for dicks, both tiny and neither one locked.

They had locks, but the door knobs twist like a merry-go-round allowing the doors themselves just to pull open.

The boy's room had a sink on the left, just before the urinal. A mirror covered with band stickers stood above the sink, making it impossible to check your nose for the coke that didn't make it up your nostrils. One toilet is straight ahead, again covered with stickers, containing a beard of hair and piss along the bowl itself.

Twenty years of pissed on checkerboard flooring provides you with three minutes of oxygen, while one dimly lit light bulb allowed minimal visibility. If you are unfortunate enough to have to shit, you must stand on the toilet seat and fire away, while a buddy guards the door on the outside, remaining hopeful that he doesn't feel like fucking with you and walking away. Always an adventure, no doubt about it.

It was early in the morning on a particular day, one which included a show at "The Clam Hut". I came to, and then proceeded to ring up Beau on his house line. I knew he was off the previous night and figured he would be in every mood to start our journey towards inevitable chaos. I was hopeful that he got a couple of hours sleep at least and also held out hope that he had some of whatever he was on left for me. Painkillers, ecstasy, blow, or anything else would suffice, I mean hell, I'm not too picky, especially in the early morning hours.

"He,LLLLLLLLLLLLLLLO?" he answered, in his usual timid, uneasy voice. Many of his sentences ended as if they were questions, when they weren't. Quite comical, but also very fucking annoying at times. On this occasion I was all too pleased to hear his funky delivery and from the second I heard his voice I knew he was ready for whatever the day had in store for us, and what a fucking day it would be!

I spent the previous day mapping out the details for every hour leading up to the time we were due to hit the stage at eleven o'clock that night. Percocets at noon, Xanax and valium at four, and then vicodin from the snaggle-toothed black cat I worked with, with booze filling all intervals. Finally at nine o'clock that night my boy Tony would meet us at the "Clam" with a chunk of the best cocaine to hit our area in a while.

That was my plan.

"Alright Beau, I'll be over at nine o'clock. We'll go have breakfast at the beach and I'll catch you up as far as what the hell's going to happen today.

Beau then told me about a drug filled evening he spent with some eighteen year old little honey the night before, and how she thought he was the coolest cat around. He said he *tried* saving some pills for me but couldn't quite hold out, also, he was sorry.

The funny thing is I know he sincerely tried to save me some. His intentions were always to hold some for me, but unless someone strapped him in a straightjacket it was impossible. Anyone who's ever played the drug scene can relate to having good intentions, and then proceeding to piss all over them as the evening rolled on. Hell, that's part of the deal. I, me, mine. Fuck you, fuck tomorrow. As long as there's money left, and drugs to be had, tomorrow can wait, you dig?

I had quite a night of booze and pills myself the night before. As I hit the shower I caught a glimpse of myself in the mirror. Damn I looked like shit. Raccoon-eyed with all kinds of random bumps and bruises scattered about my face and no idea how they got there. The last thing I remembered was having a cigarette out on my back deck and crawling into bed with my girlfriend upstairs. I tried rolling her over for a while without any luck, and then took some sleeping pills.

I got out of the shower and called my girl, Christi. She asked me if I was alright. Before I could ask what happened, she told me I was yelling at her at about two in the morning. I ran out of the room screaming and fell down the stairs. She tried to help me up but I declined belligerently. Well, that explains it. Sounds about right.

Fuck it. Today's all about the band. I'll deal with her later or maybe I won't. It really didn't faze me at all. I hit my truck, popped two vicodins, and put on some "Brianjonestownmassacre". "Wisdom" played first. I was off to the Colonel's.

I pulled into Beau's driveway around nine. His front door was open as usual and his grandmother gave me a nod while pointing upstairs. I walked into

Beau's room and found a half smoked joint on the floor amidst all the rubble which entombed his room. Beau began to speak.

"Check this out man!" he pulled from his closet a genuine World War II Colonel's get up. The shirt, the jacket, the pants, a scarf, and even a pair of flying goggles. It was perfect. "I'll be wearing this for the show tonight," he happily stated, while passing me the remnants of the joint. Of course he would be. He found it at a Thrift Store for forty bucks, a steal. Naturally I would have to get something outlandish to wear as well, so we picked up a half drunken bottle of Jack Daniels stuck to floor and headed out to the thrift shop.

I love going there. Such beautiful relics lay in wait. I was looking for a polyester long sleeved shirt with a giant collar. Mostly everything in this particular store was neatly organized, so after twenty minutes of browsing I figured I wouldn't find anything that day. The Colonel appeared out of nowhere with a long-sleeved, white, flowered shirt containing a huge collar along with a brown leisure jacket with an even bigger collar. "Here man," said Beau, with a business like smirk on his face.

It turned out the old ladies who worked there kept new arrivals which Beau was sure to dig on the side for him, since he spent a bit of cash there. I grabbed the clothes from Beau and we headed to the cashier. Beau was making small talk with an old lady on line and soon the three of us and the cashier were conversing.

They asked what we were doing for the day, so we told them about our show that night and also that we were heading to the beach for breakfast with beers. For a moment, I looked at Beau and we almost asked them to come join us. We decided not to, and headed out to my truck.

Looking back, I wish we would have taken them out. I mean hell, they were about eighty years old and I'm sure we would have made their day. It would have been real cool to hear about the good old days. Then again, they were probably scared as hell of us. After all, it was ten in the morning and we already stunk of booze and weed. Actually, who the hell am I kidding? They were sure to have been on all kinds of prescription pills, and naturally looking to get some mimosas or Bloody Maries to kick in the drugs, no? Damn, we fucked up.

On to Seaside Heights, the ash can of the Jersey Shore. I loved going there on the days of our shows because it was never too early to start drinking alcoholically in that shit hole of a town. The bars were always jammed by ten in the morning, especially if it was raining. Deadbeat dads, construction workers, and welfare women with four kids at home always made me feel a bit better about pouring whiskey down my throat and being out of my tits wasted by noon.

Beau and I ate up the whole scene, I mean shit, we were legends as far as we could see, and so what the hell is better than getting loaded in the late morning? Jimi Hendrix and Jim Morrison reincarnated, that was our take on us.

Most of the conversation going on around the bar we were in consisted of guys bragging about chicks they never really screwed, each one trying to outdo the others with tales of conquest. Quite hilarious indeed, especially because all who caught wind of the stories knew they were bullshit, and even funnier was those who spoke knew everyone knew that every fucking word which wiggled off their wasted tongues to be horseshit, but still, it went on.

In the corner of the bar, holding up the friggin walls sat a rather large tree trunk of a woman, whose neatly trimmed beard rounded off her catcher's mitt like face. As she polished off each fistful of booze she began to have a conversation with herself. With her volume getting louder as each glass of vodka went down. Next to her, and by this I mean four stools away on each side of her, were groups of cats who were feverishly brokering some drug deals. Bits of their conversation resonated in my ears and the look of anticipation on their faces allowed me to know who was getting close to closing a deal. Most sat for a bit, stood up, and sat back down with their arms like jackhammers smashing against the bar waiting for a phone call with instructions on where to meet the man.

One by one people got the call, and grins erupted over their faces. The tension and pressure slowly eased from the bar with each call, like a junkie floating off to heaven as each unit of heroin tickles his veins. Finally, my phone rang.

"My brother from another mother." Paulie always greeted me with that, and as each word hit my ears I could feel every milligram of percocet massaging my spine.

I met Paulie while working at a warehouse in Brick, New Jersey. He was a contractor who I saw every day, as he would come in and get material for his jobs. He was of course Italian, and judging by everyone else's reaction who worked with me, I knew he had the goods. Everyone surrounded him like a pack of rats. My best guess puts him at fifty years old, although one never really knows for certain, based on drugs and their multiplying effect on the body both physically and mentally.

Initially I was buying thirty milligram percocets from another cat that worked with me, but I quickly cut him out and went straight to Paulie, as it became obvious that everyone got their shit from him. Man, those little blue, mescaline looking like dots did quite a number on me. Out of all the painkillers I've ever taken these would have to be at the top of my list of favorites. Oxycontins had shit on them, whether snorting or just swallowing, I mean nothing came close to these little fuckers.

Being a businessman in all senses of the word, Paulie didn't like strangers getting a glimpse of him, and wisely so. I told him I was in Seaside drinking, so he told me to meet him at an Italian Deli about twenty minutes from where Beau and I were. As I hung up the phone it was my turn to grin with gloat as others around the bar gazed at me with envy. I smiled at Beau as we drank another whiskey for the road, tipped the bartender rather nicely for being a good nurse to us, and headed down the boardwalk to my truck floating, as if being pulled by strings.

The clock said one o'clock. I began to brief Beau on the business ahead as we flew over the bridge which separates Seaside from Toms River, with the beautiful Barnegat Bay brightly displaying diamond like glitters across her rippling tide on either side of us. We agreed that I would drop him off down the road from the deli where Paulie would be. I assured him that I wouldn't be long, knowing I was lying as the words flowed confidently from my mouth. I stopped at a liquor store and let him out; knowing at the very least he could get himself a bottle while he waited, and so he did. Beau understood the deal, with Paulie not wanting to get involved with strangers, as of course we both had been in similar situations countless times during our time on the drug train.

If there was ever such a thing as an honest drug dealer it was Paulie. I would call him a thousand times and during each conversation he told me that when he got hooked up, he'd call me, and he meant it. I realized later that he always seemed to hook up around the first of every month. Through a mutual friend I learned that Paulie got his pills from several old ladies, and by old I mean around eighty. He would buy all of their pain meds for triple what they paid for them and each side was happy. Man, what a fucking gig that must have been for him.

The thing I liked most about Paulie is also what I hated most about him: He always hooked me up with pills, but only a certain amount, and naturally, never enough in my eyes. With many people promised pills from him he rationed them out so everyone could have a taste, rather than the usual first come first serve policy. Looking back, because of his unorthodox method, I'm sure he saved my life. Hell, as it was I took three at a time even though he would only sell me twelve. That's twelve, divided by Buck, Beau, and me, with Buck only getting two of course. I'd have bought fifty if I could.

I pull up to the deli and Paulie's eating a chicken parm out of the back of his van. Friggin guy's a trip man, cool with everything that's going on and nothing but a smile tattooed about his face. It was always genuine too, no bullshit.

I sat down next to him in the van as he pulled out the bottle o' perks. He dumped twelve in my hand and I pleaded for more in vain. It was cool, hell, it had to be. Short of stabbing him and taking the whole fucking bottle that was all I was getting. Now, I can't say that thought never crossed my mind, but Paulie was the kind of guy you didn't cross, if you know what I mean.

We sat for thirty minutes talking about all kinds of stuff: the Yankees, the old crew from the tile shop- about who from there was going into rehab and who was coming out. And like always I invited him to come out to our show knowing that he wouldn't due to his "work" and family obligations. It's funny how work and family obligations bind most people to them. I'm just now figuring that one out.

As I shook his hand he reminded me to be careful, and to have a great show. At that moment I remembered Beau was waiting so I sped off. God Bless Paulie.

I arrived to the heartwarming sight of love: Colonel Von Bozwell had one hand around a brown bag of Jack Daniels and the other up against the car of two chicks, who combined were maybe thirty five. Yeah, Beau had a way with the young girls. Now, personally, I never saw him close the deal with any of these chickadees, but I do believe him when he told me the stories, that lucky prick. The girl who was driving gave Beau her number and a kiss, and so she went, out of our lives one last time, forever.

As for Beau, he jumped in my truck and popped three magical pills washing them down with some Jack and then passed me the bottle. I was thirsty.

We were due to pick up more pills in an hour, so we headed towards that destination, towards good old Bricktown, Bricktucky as we dubbed it. The name just sounds cool, it had nothing to do with any similarities to the South, it just flows you see.

We had to stop for a few cold beers as I had to prepare myself for the undesirable task I had to perform in order to get more pills. We needed some

Xanax and valium in order to get some sleep after the long night of going "uptown" which lied ahead.

After sitting at the bar for an hour, writing down our set list for the show, I got the call. Our "friend" Jenny was leaving the pharmacy and she told me to be at her place in an hour. "Better get me a shot of Jaeger Beau. I gotta go see Jen," I said, like a kid whose dog was shot, and he was on his way to its funeral. After finishing my drink I told Beau I'd return in an hour.

"Have a good time," he said, in the most sarcastic way possible, in a way a *real* Colonel would tell his soldier, as he sent him off on a suicide mission. That motherfucker!

I knew Jenny for a while, and if there's one thing that changed about her, it was everything, the whole package. This once skinny, sexy, pin-up girl fell down the ladder and landed directly into a butter basted basket of swine. Holy fuck she was HUGE now! With two kids, no more coke or heroin, and an absolute hatred of her self, I don't have to tell you how unhappy I was that I had to hump her. But I *had* to.

A few years prior, the two of us went at it like dogs and it was fantastic. I'd meet up with her, we'd screw, and then go to the pharmacy and I'd have all of her pills at my disposal. It was an arrangement I was thrilled to be a part of it. My how things had changed.

I got to her place, and the terms of our deal were spoken out, the x-rated version, in full detail. Not only did I have to screw her, but it was also required of me to go down *there* for a while, on my own, with no adult supervision. Was it worth it? Ten valium and ten Xanax?

After weighing out the pros and cons of accepting or rejecting the deal, I reluctantly went in to the bedroom and did my business. Fucking Beau, sitting at the bar, laughing it up I'm sure. Oh hell, at least we'd sleep tonight.

The worst part of the transaction was not the sex. It wasn't even going down town on her, although both sucked tremendously. It was having a cigarette with her afterwards, as I waited for her to hand over the prize. I had to relive the whole nauseating experience, while she smiled and sucked on a smoke, like a gargoyle perched on a pile of shit, looking over her tasty meal. Man, the things I've done for the greater good of the band.

I need to say more about this experience.

I recall going to the beach with my mother when I was six years old. We were enjoying some sun at Manasquan New Jersey's exquisite shore line. I went to get some ice cream with my older brother, or so I thought he was coming with me. I turned around to find him because he had the cash and I was craving that delicious toasted almond ice cream bar that only seemed to be available to me when we went to this particular beach. Wow, how fucking great they were!

Anyhow, my brother was nowhere to be found. I screamed out for him, to no avail. Son-of-a-bitch I was all alone. Briefly I was calmed down at the sight of the first perfect set of titties I'd seen during my short existence on this planet.

I wandered around forever, my virgin eyes a bit perplexed at what I saw. There were all kinds of strange people lying on the beach, listening to shitty music I might add. The women in their bikinis seemed awfully hairy, and I distinctly remember dry heaving at the sight of one of the larger ones.

Finally, my mother found me hysterically crying. She calmed me down, and then got me a toasted almond and all was well.

When I went down on Jenny I felt EXACTLY as I did on the beach that day: lost, perplexed, and plenty of gagging was going on. Generally speaking, I like to think I know what I'm doing when a woman allows me a taste of her sweetness. To this day I've never been tugged at to stop, so, again, I assume I'm doing at least an adequate job.

In this case, however, I couldn't differentiate which part of her I was working on, so I spent three minutes tops down in the abyss, holding up my end of the deal, then came up quickly, like a scuba diver whose oxygen tank was empty. I climbed on top of the great beast and entered what I though was the entrance, although who knows if I was actually inside or not. Even if I wanted to, I knew I wouldn't be able to cum, as the alcohol, pills, and scenery about me rendered my junk useless, so after what I considered to be an acceptable length of time, probably a minute or two, I just stopped. I didn't even pretend to finish, I just got up, ran to the bathroom to scrub myself down, puke, and made sure I didn't see myself in the mirror.

Jenny sent me on my way with a sack full of pills. I jumped in my truck and swallowed a couple of Xanax in order to get over the traumatic endeavor I'd just endured. I've never served I this country's military, but you bet your ass I consider myself a war veteran.

Returning to the bar I found the Colonel was holding a gram of coke that he scored from some random cat floating through the bar. He told me it was a purple heart to commemorate my victorious mission and off to the toilet we ran.

We were at one of these corporate chain restaurants whose name I won't mention because, fuck them. The bathroom was impeccable with two stalls and two stand-up pissers. Beau and I entered one stall and dumped the little plastic baggie on the back of the toilet. One gram equals two lines, especially when you only have one. A lightning bolt straight to the brain for each of us was exactly what we needed.

Walking out of the bathroom towards our drinks, my body was jumbled up, trying to figure out how to feel. Everything was happening so slowly, as the camera in my brain was filming left to right, capturing every intricate detail upon the faces of the night. It was at this moment that I realized how fucked up I was. I must have swallowed the rest of the beautiful blue perks sometime during the previous hour because I couldn't find them. Maybe it was when I took the snorkel out of jenny's ass, who knows.

In any event, they were gone and we would need more for the pain we couldn't feel yet. I called over the bartender and Beau and I slammed down two Heinekens. Next stop, the lumber yard where I worked, where Black Kirby was holding some vicodins.

I decided to jam out to some "Beatles", "Sgt. Pepper's" to be precise, as we began the trek across town to see the man. To me the most incredible part of the album is twenty seven seconds in to "Lovely Rita". Toilet paper is blown over a comb, producing a sound not heard before or since. I remember the story Lennon and McCartney told regarding this experience. The had a studio hand shop all day for toilet paper, as each different brand produced it's own unique sound. After an entire afternoon experimenting, they finally got the sound they craved.

While the song played, my body tickled with excitement, feeling like a lady with long, brown wavy hair arrived to massage my spine from the inside. She was playing the upright Bass on my bones with her strong fingers, and each movement along its neck made my feet tingle. That was the feeling I was chasing all day. When I looked over at Beau I could tell he was diggin it too.

This day was turning out to be one of those rare ones, where everyone happened to come through for us at the same time. Scoring drugs was a full time occupation, and with three different cats coming through in the same day, I felt extremely fortunate. It's like going to a bar and sitting next to a hot, young, drunk blonde chick. You still had to work for a little while but it's still *real* easy.

I called Kirby and informed his dumb black ass that I was on my way. He told me the same lame shit as always: I'll be in the yard man, meet me out there.

Ordinarily I would have argued with him for a while, insisting he'd meet me at the realtors office next to the lumber yard, but because I was enjoying my spinal rub I didn't give a shit. The only problem would be Beau. On a previous trip there to score from Kirby, I caught some shit from the guys because he waited in the car. Since my reason for going there, as far as they knew, was to hang out and bullshit for a bit, it didn't jive, so Beau would have to come inside this time.

We pulled in, and Beau fell out of the truck, creating quite a scene to all the customers standing around. I helped him up and we staggered inside. He reminded me of Tommy Chong in "Up in Smoke", when he kept falling, knocking over the drums due to some over indulgence.

I made some small talk with the salesmen in the office for a bit, and then walked out to meet Kirby in the yard, leaving Beau in there to entertain everyone. Apparently he had them rolling on the floor with his antics, struggling to keep himself on his feet while slurring his drug and booze infested words.

I've come a long way in my relationships with black people, but Kirby brought out the worst in me because he always played the race card when we worked together. I was the guy who told the cats in the yard what to do, and usually I went to him. He claimed it was because he was black, but truth be told I liked the way he got shit done, and he was fast. The fact that I bought pills from him also made it convenient to go converse with him as we exchanged the cash for the goods.

There he was, atop the biggest forklift in the yard, with all three of his upper teeth smiling away. Kirby's a dead ringer for the black dude on the cover of "The Rolling Stones" "Exile on Main St." album. A giant head explodes from his shoulders, with arms that drag alongside of him, knuckles on the ground.

You see, Kirby and I had an understanding with each other, which started from the first day I met him. He called me a WOP as I was giving him an assignment. Fortunately for both of us no one was around, and at this time I responded to him matter-of-factly: "Listen nigger, if you want to start out like this I'm fine with it. I must tell you though, your life means absolutely nothing to me, so if you feel it necessary to carry on this way, proceed. And just so you're clear, I called you NIGGER, not nigga! Here's a list of materials I need, so get the fuck to it BOY!

From that day on, we got along okay for the most part, as well as could be expected anyway.

"Alright Kirby, what do you got for me today?" I asked, as I finally arrived at his forklift.

"Wull, I got twenty 7.5 milligram vikes, but I'm not selling them all to you," he responded, knowing in fact he actually *was* going to sell me them all.

"Okay great. Here's seventy five for all of them, and don't give me any shit about it 'cause I need to get going." I demanded.

I grabbed the plastic baggie containing twenty vicodins and was on my way. Out front I grabbed Beau and we left, proceeding out of the gate in a flash. I'm not sure if I said goodbye to the boys inside, but I can say with certainty that Beau hadn't, as he was already by my truck when I got there, holding up the front end as one would do when annihilated.

I called Buck reluctantly, knowing he'd give me shit about already being carelessly twisted. We agreed to meet at "The Clam" for nine o'clock, with each of us bringing up our own equipment. As he hung up with me, Beau and I realized that unless Tony hooked us up with some blow before the show started, it would be impossible for the two of us two stand up without assistance let alone play an hour long set. We each swallowed two vicodins without liquid as best as we could. Where the fuck was my water?

I called Tony to get the usual bullshit response. "Yeah we're all good for tonight, I'll be there by nine," he told me, both of us kind of chuckling about it.

There's a sliding scale as far as how late the man's going to be, based on what he's selling you. If it's weed he's holding for you, expect to sit around for an extra half and hour or so; Any kind of pills, an extra hour; Cocaine, hell, if you get it two hours late you've done exceptionally well. I've been on both sides of the drug deal and I know this time table to be extremely accurate.

As far as chicks for the night, there would be several coming to see us. Jessica from Brooklyn was making the hour drive down. Now this girl knew how to party man. A few months earlier, before I really knew her, she came down to visit Buck, who lived with me at the time. The two of them had some kind of relationship together, though I'm sure they never screwed.

When she arrived at our place on a Friday, Buck was out somewhere. She had a jar of coke and offered me a bump. The next thing I remember it was Sunday morning, a dozen empty bottles of red wine were on the floor (yellow tail I believe), and Buck walked past us with a look of disgust as Jessica and I were naked on the couch in the living room.

Samantha, some broad form Northern Jersey, the daughter of my mother's boss, would also be coming. I tried like hell to get in her pants countless times without success. Her legs stretch up about seven feet and attach to an ass worthy of being displayed in a museum. Perfect tits which perked upwards like Hershey's Kisses had broken many necks I'm sure as she strolled down the streets of the cities she dwelled. Her face, however, led my eyes directly back to her tits and ass. She was a great one for the drunkard alright, so if all else failed, at least I could mess around with her after the show.

Jocelyn would also be there, licking her chops, seeking out the next poor bastard she could commit adultery with, and various other thirty year old gals from my tanning salon were coming, bringing with them an appetite and thirst for all things nasty.

Funny thing about thirty and over women: It's been my experience, since turning twenty one and taking my first one home, that *all* of them love when you go in through their out door. (Pull it up a notch! I remember my buddy Joe Simon after we founded the thirty plus club)

Of course Beau had promised some fresh eighteen year olds from the supermarket where he worked would be there, but I was miles away from getting excited over this promise, only to be disappointed again. Beau usually ended up with the hottest chick anyway, and without much effort I must add. Colonel Van Boswell, the legend.

Beau and I returned to his place to load up our equipment and change for the show. Usually I wash the clothes I buy at the thrift shop before I wear them, but time didn't permit this, so I put on my new polyester shirt and brown leisure jacket and waited outside for Beau. And there he was, dawning his recently purchase Colonel Attire, drunk as hell, looking like he just returned from the Battle of Midway. Beautiful. Perfect. Fitting. Off we went.

The ride up to "The Clam" that evening was perhaps the most frightening trip of all time for me. Most times when I was driving, nothing bothered me. I couldn't stay in one lane for more than a few seconds, so I had to employ a technique taught to me years before on a return trip to Jersey from New York: The Garden State Parkway has three lanes. So if you get in the middle one and begin to drift left or right, all you have to do is put your blinker on in whichever direction you swayed, and then hustle back to the middle.

Thirty minutes of this and I was a broken man. For as much as the "Clam" was a shit hole, when we arrived it was a palace, a body of water in the desert for my disheveled soul. Beau and I stumbled out of the truck and tried to carry our guitars and all inside. Tommy greeted us at the entrance and said something like, "What the fuck guys," or "Not Again!" or some shit like that, and then he got some cat from inside to help carry everything in and onstage for us. Man, he smelled like he wiped his ass with his beard.

To the bar, straight to the bar goddamn it. Two Heinekens and two double shots of bourbon for the Colonel and I. Buck walked in without saying a word to us, as apparently Tommy briefed him on our condition. He was furious, and I felt it.

One by one, people arrived as Beau and I remained frozen at the bar, paralyzed by gallons of booze and fistfuls of pills devoured throughout the day. Where the fuck was Tony? It was now nine thirty and he wasn't answering the phone, surprise, surprise. No way can I play like this. Where are my fingers? Fuck you Buck, I know you're pissed but what the fuck are you gonna do about it? After concluding this conversation with myself, Tommy tapped me on the shoulder.

"Hey man, the second band cancelled, so you're on in ten minutes. Are you going to be able to play?" he asked.

I told him I was fine, that Beau and I were fine, but pleaded with him for an extra fifteen minutes or so, allowing my friend Tony to arrive as he had never seen us jam before. Tommy's no fool; he knew what I was waiting on.

A browse throughout the place revealed ridiculous amounts of people, mostly chicks, and they looked *good*. Buck came over to Beau and I and we all reviewed the set list. What a feeling of helplessness it was, while I studied the songs we were to play, knowing we would suck if Tony didn't arrive soon with the sweet taste of cocaine. With one eye closed Beau told us he couldn't play, as his legs wouldn't move and his fingers were locked shut. Buck got loud, and rightfully so, saying that we better be fucking ready or he was through with the both of us. He was quite sincere too; I can assure you of that. The whole scene was fucking fantastic though; sex, drugs, and rock n'roll, you know?

"Alright, you guys are on," Tommy interrupted us. "Let's go!"

I walked towards the stage, stumbled, and then grabbed Beau and we fell to the ground, with all kinds of shit from the floor stuck against my face. As I sat up, Tony was walking in, Santa himself had arrived! "Alright, Tommy, give us ten fucking minutes and we'll blow this place to Holy Hell!" I screamed

I paid Tony's admission, and then Beau, Tony, and I sprinted to the disgusting yet so pleasant looking toilet, and I screamed at Tony to hack out two of the biggest cannons he could imagine. "Hurry the fuck up man!" I screamed, as I could hear Buck onstage pounding away on his kick drums. "Let's go motherfucker!" Beau hammered down his line and instantaneously I could hear the crazy guitar going off inside his mind. Just before I vacuumed up my line with my nose, I had an overwhelming feeling that everything was going to be alright. I thought of all the young bitches, and old ones too, that were waiting for us, how I was going to have my way with every single one of them in one way or another.

The two giant squanks of blow we fired up our noses affected us like this: A deaf guy is standing up, with his arms outstretched on a table, as instructed by his doctor who assures him he can teach him to speak. The doctor grabs a broomstick and runs toward the deaf man from across the room, then drives it so far up his ass that his prostate gets splinters. "AAAAAYYYY!!" the deaf man screams, not minding the pain so much, in fact pleased as peach that he fucking said *something*, now ready to tear up the fucking world.

Beau and I screamed so damn loud with amazement, just like that deaf motherfucker. We faced each other, and then suddenly Beau punched me in the jaw, knocking me back into the wall. We traded punches for a minute, letting all the adrenaline, very much coke-induced adrenaline flow throughout.

We then stormed out onto the stage, and with three clicks of Buck's sticks it was on. "I like the bright lights baby, I'm so addicted crazy, I'm in with the out crowd lately, we just get up and go," Beau howled, as we opened with "Equalizer," playing an already speedy tune practically double time.

The collective screams from the crowd after that first song reminded me exactly why I love playing music. Buck looked at me with his "right on brother" nod, while Beau was devouring the row of little chicks up front with his eyes, and all was well. Somewhere through his Rasputin-like beard I saw Tommy smiling. It was like that man, the only thing that mattered in the end was the music, the girls too, but hell, when we jammed balls out everything always went so smoothly.

The next day we all met up for drinks, Buck, Beau, and I. Beau filled us in on his little escapade with one of the teeny boppers he screwed in her car, outside of "The Clam." Buck was just pleasantly pleased at another Sungroove Liberation Revolution show gone good. All was right with the world.

Thanks guys. Thanks Tommy. Thanks Tony, sweet carrier of cocaine.

Oh yeah, thank *you*, Jessica.

IV.   The Rusty Door Knob

Buck, Beau, and I arrived in Brooklyn around eight o'clock for our debut at "The Rusty Door Knob" sometime between February 2002 and June 2005, another one of Billy the Hat's joints. The doors opened and immediately we entered the nostril of the night, with an awe-inspiring sense of comfort about us, and fervor which rivaled only being second on line for the shitter, knowing the cat in there was slicing out a piece of heaven just for you.

Long, straight, amber hair she had, standing around six foot, with a black tank top on and magical arms steadily slinging booze to the patrons at the bar which already was four deep. Her name was Rebecca Reardon and she was perhaps the most pristine looking woman I'd ever seen, and the fact that she was our bartender for the night only heightened my sense of rapture for her. I would certainly see her a little later.

It was only about fifty feet wide inside, the bar being on the left, with tables and chairs arranged so cozily along the right side they practically sent personalized invitations to all who glanced at them demanding you take a load off.

A hallway running along the bar seemed to stretch on for a while, dimly lit but quite enticing while the stage was off centered right three feet from the floor and plenty wide. Yeah, you could smell the coke in this joint alright.

Two bathrooms, one for balls, one for holes were down the hall on the left side and ten more paces led you outside in the back and holy fuck what a scene slapped the shit out you as you hit it! Picnic tables and grills engulfed a back yard like mine at the Jersey Shore, about two hundred square feet in all. Chicks were plentiful, and Billy the Hat himself was flipping burgers with a fat ass stogie rotting right out of his mouth. Booze and city creatures ruled the night, with sounds of "The Pixies" echoed around the speakers so carefully spread out in this little paradise so perfectly.

Amongst the spread of folks, I spotted the douche bag. Many times this was me, and looking back I must admit it turned out to be me, however, every cell of this cat's being screamed out, "I'm the cocksucker!" and at that instant the night held a sort of *reckoning on the horizon* type vibe. Excellent.

I learned that this dude's band was hitting the stage just before we did, so being the opportunist that I am, I calculated that I had a couple of hours to get obliterated before I needed to figure out just how in fact this motherfucker and I would be involved on this particular evening.

Buck, Beau, and I strolled back inside with a sort of slow motion feel, again glancing around and soaking up the scene. Colonel Von Boozewell was first up to the bathroom, playing the role of cut man as he did so well. We had scored an eight ball from some clown from Beau's work, and surprisingly it was pretty damn good. I would have loved to film the Colonel chopping up some lines while we were in these random, shitty bathrooms we've been in through the years. I mean shit; I've obviously seen him hundreds of times when we were at my house, displaying text book form while slicing, but to see him in the shitter alone, with time restrictions, and realizing the end result to be three perfectly powdered cannons is worth at least a pinky toe to me.

The line to get into the toilet consisted of two degenerate cocksuckers just like us, and the people coming out were definitely indulging in sweet tastes themselves, fondling their noses and eyes wide open as if their eyelids were cut off. The thing is, although everyone was holding blow, we had to play brainless for a while, being careful no to be crazily blatant.

Being a professional cokehead is a craft misunderstood by anyone who hasn't lived it. Of course looking back it's clear we were out of our fucking minds; however, to live that life requires an ability to adapt and overcome countless situations in order to maximize one's consumption. Any hesitation or overlooking could create a tremendous downsizing of the amount of blow one would consume.

Man this pen blows. I'm using a pilot G2-07 rather than my usual G2-10.

Two sweet lines a piece in the toilet ignited the evening for Buck, Beau, and me, also prompted a trip to the bar to see the nurse. I handed "Brianjonestownmassacre's" "Take it From the Man" to the tremendously sculpted Rebecca and asked her to play it. She did. "We'll have three double Glen Fitich and three Heinekens baby," I said to her, as the first coke induced drip came down my nose, numbing my tongue.

I turned and surveyed the crowd and layout and couldn't wait to hit the stage, knowing that we were going to set that fucking room on fire with our sound. The Colonel was in fine form, having achieved the ideal cocktail mix of painkillers, booze, and blow. Buck was deep in trance, silent, but exuding an air of confidence about him that set me up in a feeling of delight. It was as if someone had painted me on a cloud because they knew they couldn't be there, you dig?

It was then that I saw the douche bag tuning up his bass, which immediately stirred up some anger due to the fact that now he was my rival, my counterpart of the night. Beau, sensing my disgust, brought another bourbon to me and handed off the sack of blow. I explained to him my mindset, on how I felt I needed to kick the hell out of this dickhead, just for being a dickhead. Now, I'm certainly not an imposing figure, standing five foot six on my *best* day, weighing around one fifty, one forty after three days of blow. The thing is, no matter who I was up against I always felt like I had an advantage. Usually the booze and drugs convinced me of this, but shit, as long as the poor motherfucker had an Adam's apple I could rip out, I'd be alright.

Unsurprisingly, Beau assured me of his willingness to assist me in *any* way he could, so, with that in mind I swiftly hustled off to the bathroom for another treat, grabbing Buck on my way.

Since I was the cut man on this run I dumped out the balance of the bag and proceeded to chop out three rock filled mammoths for me and my boys. I couldn't even be slick walking out of the bathroom due to the tremendous head rush and also the little pebbles falling from my nose, trying to escape to freedom before I sucked them back up. I passed the rolled up twenty to the Colonel and headed out back for a smoke.

Billy the Hat was finished cooking and was sitting with a pack of folks telling drug induced stories from the previous evening. Apparently some jerk off fell off the stage mid-way through his band's set causing massive blood loss from his head. Yeah, sounded familiar.

The first time I heard the Hat's stories I immediately dismissed them as horseshit, not allowing my brain to even attempt to enjoy them. After a while, however, they were so ridiculously full of holes I found it more enjoyable to accept them as fact and inquire for more details.

As the crowd of fools began fading away, I sat down next to him for a one on one. I told him I needed blow, as if he didn't know, so he handed me a hundred sack and a fat one at that. Beau and Buck joined us and we all began romancing the night. Beau began with this: "Man, we need to expand our horizons and start getting out to new cities to spread the word on our movement- The Sun groove Liberation Revolution". Too many dog shit bands with no soul, lacking any hint of what the fucking world's really about. We need to hand out some truth, carefully capturing chaos and packaging it in a way even the simplest of minds can understand."

Buck chimed in: How 'bout this man. Just try to remember the fucking set list tonight, alright Socrates?

The Hat started laughing.

Buck had a way of smacking Beau and I back down to Earth at times. On some of these occasions, we'd get pissed, Beau more than I, but as for this time we felt so goddamn good it didn't matter what he said. Shit, he could have told me he shot and killed my dog and I'd have given him a hug with a smile, thanking him all the way for ridding me of such a terrible thing.

Man, I loved these two guys. I mean the way we felt about each other is difficult to convey. It's a bit like being brothers, but stronger, as if they were my kids, and I was their kid, all at the same time. I'd have killed any motherfucker who caused them pain, and any bullets in their direction would have had to go through me first. I still feel this way today, perhaps more than ever. If I never see them again they'll remain the two closest cats to my soul, and every time I play my bass, no matter who I'm jamming with, I think of the mighty fucking Sungroove Liberation Revolution first. Any songs, lyrics or music that I write now will take a back seat to those we'd written together. Man, I miss them.

Ah, the Hat's blow was always best. Of course it was stepped on, but it's like the cat who stepped on it took his shoes off when he was making our bag up. Smooth, very little paranoia and a numbing effect you could spot on someone from across the room.

After a nice taste I hurried over to the bar to see that tall angel Rebecca for some medicine. She saw how tweaked I was and asked if she might have a little bump. Of course I said yes with a smile, at least I believe I was smiling, but you see I couldn't feel my face at all. She poured me a fat bourbon on the rocks and suggested I follow her into the office for some added privacy. Um… Okay.

The office was a miniature citadel of sorts, cozy, yet very much weathered from the nights long gone bye. Two couches, big red ones with room for three a piece boxed in a terrific mirrored coffee table which contained signatures of scratches from the incredible amounts of cocaine sliced upon it over the years. Real classy it was.

And she looked *good*. I watched her tie her hair in a ponytail carefully, making sure each strand of her movie star mane was bound back allowing an uninhibited path as she bent over, diving into a line which was left there for her by someone else who came in before us.

I dropped the sack on the table and offered her a credit card so she could chop. She smiled and pulled out a razorblade with a glass straw and said, "Just give me a minute silly boy."

There was no rush in that room; almost every other time while in the city everything had to be fast, sloppy, and not too pleasant. Now I could actually relish and envision what she would be like in bed, as she carved and chopped until two perfect lines lay before us.

As she passed me the straw I noticed what an incredible ass she had, rising from the table so fluidly. When I finished my line she grabbed me and extended her appreciation with a kiss, and then lit me a cigarette. I must say, out of all the chicks I've pleasured and been pleasured by at our shows, this kiss felt better than anything those other broads ever did to me. I knew that that was all that was going to happen between us, and I'm sure anything more would have taken away its beauty. Christ, what a woman.

Reality returned as we left the office, as I ran into the very douche bag himself. He gave me some shit, verbal shit, so I winked at him. Apparently he didn't appreciate that at all, as I heard mumble some kind of caveman shit as he walked by. "I'll see you soon," I said to myself.

I noticed a rather homely looking broad follow him to the bar and when she kissed him I knew at that moment I was going to fuck her at some point that night just to piss this motherfucker off and then the show would really take some turns. Roughly twenty minutes remained before this dick and his shit eating band hit the stage, so I figured I'd lay low with Buck and Beau (if you consider laying low firing bourbon and cocaine down like junkies) and stare down this cocksmoker's girl to clearly announce my intentions to her, of fondling her ass a bit later.

Billy the Hat was all kinds of fucked up, falling down as he came in from the Garden of Eden out back, dropping a hundred sack from his hand as he hit the floor (unfortunately for us he picked it up). The night was on man, chaos and treachery filled the air. Beau was romancing some Asian chick and Buck had his arms around a short, cute little honey, and I was fixated on douche bag's girl from across the room, and she began to smile right back at me. Yes, The Sungroove Liberation Revolution was riled the hell up now, liquored up, and flying high. Be patient little girl, your time is near.

The cat's band hit the stage. Well, well, well, little pussy's playing with a pick. Fag, soulless puke, maybe I'd stick it in your girl's ass now. Amazingly though his band was pretty decent. A power trio with some cat named Jonesy wailing away on guitar, resembling Jerry Garcia in his early days, before his beard went gray. Dude on drums caught Buck's ear right from the get, with his chops perfectly bouncing off the ceiling and walls like a pinball unleashed on the streets. But all focus for me was on the shit stick playing bass with a pick.

Now, I'm sure I get some pretty damn screwy looking images on my face when I'm playing my bass, in fact, I've been told I do many times, but it's genuine every time. This cocksucker was manufacturing every little expression he gave, and I'm sure he practiced in the mirror for many an hour, the prissy little prick..

Any guy holding a bag of blow in a club is at least assured of getting any girl into the toilet when the moment's right. About thirty minutes into the band's set I knew this stormy looking girl was ready for a line.

I got up next to her and told her to follow me for a bump. Like a vulture pouncing on a meal she was on my ass right quick. At this point what crossed my mind was whether or not I'd have whiskey dick or not thus being unable to plow this little whore in two minutes or less.

I followed her into the ladies room and quickly realized there was a lock on the door. Strange, unfair, how the chicks room more times than not had a lock while the guys' was always broken. Fucking animals we are.

I propped her ass up on the sink, and guided her feet onto the toilet seat. From there I doused the back of the toilet with enough coke for two fatties. Roughly forty-five seconds of chop time was all I needed, so I handed her the rolled up twenty offering her first dibs. Slow-mo appeared as she rose from her crouch after taking the hit passing me the bill. I dove into my line with a fury and fired up my fix.

No bullshit now. No kissing. Just business. I dropped her pants and threw her against the wall with her arms on the door and ass arched high in the air. No whiskey dick, no problems, (no condom either, thank god no backlash) just two minutes of rage filled action until finally finishing. A quick wash of the hands and out the door we went.

The first image upon my exit was priceless. The Colonel and Buck were working on two fine young fillies that were fresh as strawberries. Buck's was a tall one, with plenty of fine meat on her in all the right spots. Straight jet black hair engulfed her face, with each strand around her eyes swaying back and again like a sun flower left to right in the wind, gusting, but not too strong, leaving much to the imagination. Twenty-four solid years she must have been.

Von Bozwell on the other hand, liked them young, hell, who doesn't. His chick had short hair, almost butch like, with a tattoo of a nun covered in blood coming up out of her shirt, which was quite colorful in its own right. Somehow, she accumulated nineteen years despite being a veteran of sex riots, self inflicted of course. Yeah, she appeared to be the type of gal that would punch you in the face after she finished riding your knob, just before depositing a chunk of shit on your chest, and finally stealing your wallet. Good for Beau.

I shot the dickhead on bass a look of conquest and winked at him as if planting a flag with a furious fist declaring his chick for my own. She made her way out of the bathroom by then and I knew then that he understood what went on. A pause in his pick playing pussiness assured me he wasn't let's say, delighted.

To the bar for a bourbon, the good shit, double sized, iced, and smooth. Everyone around me was snorting and wiping away the drips falling from their noses, enjoying the fruits of Billy the Hat's unparalleled connections to the goods. We all understood each other; in fact many spoke openly about their quantities and of what kind of bartering could be implemented. Yeah, it was cool.

The band finished playing, meaning we were up in thirty minutes. I took a stroll out front to soak up the Brooklyn streets for a bit. About half a block from the club, I though I had to piss. You know, when your veins contain more booze than blood your body plays tricks on you regarding whether or not you have to go at times.

I saw a couple walking out of a brownstone, seemingly happy with each other, though strangely curious as far as their mannerisms showed. I asked them if I could use their bathroom, after all, pissing in public in the city carries a $250 fine, a lesson I learned leaving the subway to Yankee Stadium a few years back. They told me they didn't live there, but they were kind enough to watch for cops as I painted the building with my waste. Genuine upstanding individuals you see.

I spoke to them about the night, naturally describing only what I was into not really giving a fuck in the least for their story. I invited them to come and check out our show. Two dissimilar cats they could not have been. The chick was maybe five feet tall, with a barrel ass reminding me of plenty of evenings I had as a youth, drunk on I anything I could get my hands on and willing to fuck a snake if someone held it. Her nappy bleached blonde hair was shoulder length and filled with what can only be described as a cum bin from probably more than a few stray cocks over the previous several days.

The dude was hilarious. If I was an artist I'd have painted his portrait and made thousands from its unique images. At times he seemed around six feet from the ground while at others he bellied over like a person trying to smuggle a turkey out of the supermarket, not slickly of course, with it stuck on his back with his tight green corduroy jacket holding it in place.

His hair was uneven all around, with the left side, my left, two inches shorter than the right. An old raggedy face seemed to attach itself directly to his torso, and I swear his right ear was much bigger than the left. A bit of a limp quite noticeable hampered the chap's movement as he paced up and down the sidewalk.

We parted ways, agreeing to have a drink together at the club if they showed up. A walk back towards the club brought such a sweet surprise: Douche bag was coming towards me, having just stormed out the doors, his cronies close behind.

Now the thing was, I deserved an ass kicking. If someone mounted my chick while I was onstage I'd have jumped right off and immediately cut his throat from ear to ear, tied a knot around his head with his tongue, and then headed to the bar for a beer and a bourbon.

I figured I'd let him hit me first, making penance for my actions. And so he did, and with the impact of his fist to my jaw and my falling quickly to the sidewalk a boat load of adrenaline shot through my veins as if fired in there by Keith Richards himself. While picking myself up to my feet I noticed a decent crowd around. Buck and Beau gave me the look, announcing their readiness to me, but I quickly shook my head at them implying I was alright.

I charged at that cocksucker like the great "Bodacious" surely did at the matadors who pissed him off, grabbed a hold of him around his back and smashed the both of us into the wall of the club, brick mind you. As blood from his cock-eyed head spurted onto my face I grabbed his legs from the back just below his knees and repeatedly drove his skull into the concrete, the wall, then the sidewalk, vice-versa, and so on. Punches of coke induced rage left my hands hitting any part of him I could, usually his face, until at last he was pouring blood from every part of his head.

Obviously he had enough, so I began to walk away, glancing at the spectators around, enjoying the look of horror on the faces who witnessed this one sided affair. Buck and Beau appeared, with Buck displaying a troubled look I've never seen him have before, despite innumerable tasteless scenes I've put him through in the past. Beau, however, was quite satisfied with me, beaming a light of approval from his eyes to mine, making me feel like an anointed man who was receiving the torch from his master.

A desire for more destruction caused an about face for one last encounter with the poor bastard still lying on the ground, his buddies trying to help him collect his thoughts and brain particles. He was perfectly placed on all fours. My thoughts flashed back to gym class in 1993 when I dropped some LSD, green skulls, during school. It was third period and I was tripping my nuts off and we were playing floor hockey. I had the ball, a bright orange one, and I peered over Stefano Mirabelli's left shoulder as he was minding the goal, and it was wide open. In slow motion in my mind I snapped a wrist shot with all I had. Real time returned in my brain with Stefano's vain attempt with the glove hand to make the save. Goal motherfucker, over the shoulder glove side. That was the highlight of my trip that day with the exception of fifth period study hall in the library staring at that carpet and all its terrific patterns.

I ran towards the blood ridden half of a corpse quickly, being careful in timing my steps just right in order to kick the cocksucker right in the jaw. Slow mo upon impact and the sight of his blood coming off of my shoe into the air capped off an absolute ass kicking with the cherry on top and all, hell, even the cigarette.

At this juncture Buck himself wrapped his massive body around mine insuring my rampage would cease. There aren't many things comparable to landing a kick right on the button when the cat is totally at your mercy. I saw then exactly how big the crowd was surrounding me, so it was time to get the fuck inside and jam.

Billy the hat grabbed my arm on the way in and said, "The stage is yours whenever you guys are ready."

Without words Buck, Beau, and I returned inside and hit the bar. Damn I was thirsty. Rebecca shot me a smile, apparently seeing the blood all over me, admiring me in a twisted, yet sexy kind of way. We hit the toilet for a couple of toots, and then to the *real* stage. Beau suggested we open with "Sweet Oblivion", citing how appropriate it would be. I concurred.

We took the stage in a drunken haze and scattered about for a bit, trying to get our drinks situated so we wouldn't knock them over, though we always did. I noticed that the ass kicked cat and his band mates were in the crowd. I give him a lot of credit for sticking around man. Hell, I probably would have been long gone if I got my ass kicked like that. Actually, Beau and I would have stormed the stage and mangled the whole fucking band with whatever we could get our hands on but still I give the man credit.

Man, I remember having a feeling of complete contentment when we started playing. More times than not when we hit the stage it was more or less a countdown until we finished in order to snort another line. That night was special though. We could have played for hours.

I dedicated "Sweet Oblivion" to my new *friend* and he shot me a smile while clapping for us. From then on me and that cat were alright with each other. His girl had disappeared by then anyway, so we really had no current reason for friction between us, other than the obvious, but that was finished. Pussy has a way of causing chaos, usually welcomed by the participants. It's amazing how that three inch stripe has all power over most situations. Shit, we could probably solve many of our problems by just unleashing our finest piece of pussy on it.

Halfway through our set while jamming "Darkened Eve," Buck stopped playing because his nose started shooting blood. He grabbed a shirt that he kept by his feet, wiped himself off thoroughly, and then came back in. He couldn't have timed it better if he planned the whole thing, so, quite accidentally, each time form then on when we played that song we inserted the pause, fucking magic man.

From the stage I saw the bouncers were in a scuffle by the front door with bar stools and booze being thrown about. I loved when we were out of control on stage, and all those around were out of hand as well. I like to think we had a way of bringing out the evil side in folks, not in a murderous way, but you know, *evil*.

We closed the set with a twenty minute medley of "The Warlocks," "Shake the Dope Out" into our own "Downfall of it All." The last note of that evening still fills my soul to this day, and judging by the hat full of cash Billy the Hat handed to us from all those inside, the crowd dug it too. I liked getting paid by the crowd based on performance, I mean, if we sucked, don't give us shit man.

After some small talk with the little whores gathered at our feet, the Hat tossed me the keys to his office so the band and I could have a celebratory rail in a bit of privacy. We took our time in there, discussing the mistakes we thought we made, then realizing we actually didn't make too many of them. As I came up from table, coke all over my face, a big black bouncer barged in, not knowing we were inside. I told him to come sit with us and have a taste, and so he did.

I asked him what all the commotion was about during our set. He told me that some asshole invited two of the neighborhood's most notorious thieves to come by. They were all fucked up and started waving around knives with hopes of robbing the place, but swiftly they were *escorted* out the fucking door. He snorted up his line like a snake takes on its meal, so I left him one more fatty and we all walked out.

"By the way," I said, "Sorry 'bout bringing those two people here man," and out the door we went.

The Hat was calling us from down the hall wanting us to join him outside for a smoke and a tea. He sang our praise for a while, and then invited us to a party a few blocks away in the neighborhood. We said yes of course, especially after looking at the entourage of pussy that would be joining us.

After several more drinks the Hat locked up the club and we all proceeded out the door down the city streets to the next destination of the beautiful evening. It was more than a few blocks away, but we didn't care because the line of fine asses walking with us told us not to. I remember walking into a large colorful place packed with all sorts of people ranging from young and hot to every other imaginable combination. Vaguely I remember falling down several times, soaking my pants with blood, not knowing if it was mine or otherwise.

The next clear thought I recall was stumbling into the street and trying to find my truck. The thing about the city is there's a bit of a delay in the sunrise, what with all the tall buildings shading it you see. It looked like it was eight thirty, turned out it was ten thirty. Sounded about right.

We found my car and as I tried to open the fucking doors I saw that the key hole was mangled up. I didn't pay it any mind at the time, so I opened the passenger door and quickly sped away.

The rides home for gigs were usually the same. Beau rapidly faded into his own little world while Buck and I reviewed the goings on of the night eventually arriving at silence for the final forty five minutes or so.

Around noon we pulled up to the Colonel's house and I opened the back of the truck. Beau could never figure out how to open it, you know, because you had to hit the button, lift the window, and then open the door. Holy fuck! It was then we learned we had been robbed. My first bass, Roxanne, my queen, gone. Beau's nineteen sixty-something Fender Strat was also gone. Actually, it wasn't even his guitar, some random dude left it at his house. Oh well, fuck it, hopefully someone else would create some good shit with them now, although I'm sure some crack head pawned them both for fifty bucks. At least he got his fix though, you know? That's something I could understand so good for him.

As Beau went inside and the screen door closed behind him I heard his mother ask, "How was the show Beau?"

"It was good mom."

V. <u>Random Acts of Belligerent Boldness</u>

I fucked a troll once. I must admit it was one hell of a good time, at least for a little bit and hell, I'm writing about the terrible shit fourteen years later so an impression of some kind was evidently made.

I was away at college at a small school in Massachusetts, about forty minutes left of Boston. To be able to buy the amounts of booze and drugs I desired, I was forced to take a job in the produce section of a supermarket. Mom's cash would only go so far you know.

This little chick, I mean *little*, about four foot eight, worked in the bakery department and also went to my school. She in fact lived in my dorm on the third floor. She and I would walk back to the dorm after work; more like she followed me like a fucking junkie does anyone holding the goods.

"You're so cute. You're so cute," the little hag would always say, grabbing my fucking cheeks with pinches. I'd tell her to shut the fuck up and then pour some beer down my throat which I routinely picked up for the stroll after work. It was about two miles from work to school, most of it involving an uphill trek which was the downfall of many a student who hit the bars and had to walk that way. Guilty of that I am several times.

As you approach the school you can go one of two ways; a right turn leads you the long way around the school but offers relief as the stretch flattens out considerably. The other way went up an enormous hill through the woods, but was significantly shorter and it led right to the dorms at which we lived. Most nights on our walk back the troll and I went the way of the woods because we could stop halfway up and sit on a giant rock and proceed to finish whatever we bought for that stretch run home.

Oh yeah, our campus was a dry one. There were twenty one and over dorms but fuck that you know. Only the deadbeats stayed there. We had a pulley system to haul our booze up from behind the building which worked like an eight ball does for anyone seeking nirvana.

One night after work this little pig and I began our walk. She started immediately with her usual shit, grabbing my face and practically dry humping my leg. At this moment I decided fuck it: I'm going to give this little girl a night she will remember, for good reasons or bad I wasn't sure, probably bad but who knew man chicks are much freakier than you think. I turned around and headed into the liquor store, knowing that beer wasn't going to do it for me. Old I'll screw anything whiskey was precisely what the night called for.

Thank god for booze. After I consciously decided that I was going to have sex with a troll this chick's defects quickly multiplied. Her Raggedy Anne orange red hair shone straight into my eyes. Her neck rippled with freckles and I swear for a quick minute a giant fucking wart swallowed her nose. A slug from the jug.

We walked and passed the bottle back and forth with each gulp I took increasing my willingness to carry out the ghastly act. At the foot of woods I grabbed her and stuck my tongue violently into her mouth. Another belly full of whiskey followed.

She sat for a minute on the giant rock and I quickly grabbed her and dragged her up the hill. I didn't want to wait. I actually grew extremely excited by the shear madness of it all. At the top of the hill behind the dorm we finished the bottle and I threw it back over the way we came.

We swiftly strolled in the dorm past the front desk and disappeared into the elevator, both of us feeling quite nice inside. She lived on the third floor, me on the eighth. My floor was the only one you could smoke on with a disgusting not fit for a street dweller community smoke room at the center of it all. Perfect!

I took that little gal's arm and like a bailiff grabs a convicted man and pulled her into the smoke room dungeon locking the door behind us. Don't get me wrong here, she was into it the entire way, this ain't no criminal confession. I ripped her pants down and threw her against the ash filled table and had my way. It didn't last long, which was most definitely surprising considering the whiskey dick I was working with.

I immediately felt like shit. I vehemently screamed bloody murder prompting her to get up and get out quicker than I should have. I sat there in the little slice of shit I carved out for myself feeling as if I was violated. Goddamn those whores!

A few hours later, after sucking down ridiculous amounts of booze by myself along with firing a few not so good yet quite good lines of coke Donnie, the campus dealer and one of only eight blacks in the entire school sold me earlier that afternoon and then I set out for the third floor for another round with the little nightmare. I was already tainted so I figured what the hell, what's another dance with the devil going to hurt you know?

As I said, this coke was not so good, and while I snorted it because well, that's what I do, I also hoped it could keep me up for a little bit before the black out came. No sir. The last thing I remembered was finding the troll in the hallway sitting on the floor alone against the wall, basically passed out.

Next conscious moment I found myself being shaken violently by a fireman. He was screaming at me to get out of the dorm. A couple of cobwebs cleared and I realized I was naked, with the little leprechaun lying next to me, naked as well. I looked up at the fireman as if he were my father, hoping he'd tell me it was okay. He shook his head at me and his face expressed the grim reality of the situation.

Like every weekend, some asshole pulled the fire alarm, and as a result the firemen automatically came to investigate. They knew it was bullshit but had to do it anyway, just in case you see.

I scurried around the room looking for my clothes. The beast, who finally woke up, threw on a t-shirt and shorts and started to leave the room. Where the fuck are my clothes?

"You have to leave right now!" the fireman shouted.

Alright man. I grabbed a sheet and followed him down the stairs and out into the parking lot of the dorm. The little chick struggled to keep up. We got outside and every mother-fucker who lived in the dorm was standing there. You see the alarm keeps sounding until the entire dorm is empty, and apparently the troll and I slept through the whole ordeal only to be awoken by the forceful shakes of the fireman.

I stopped and stared onto the crowd of people, most of whom were friends of mine. I gazed at several girls who I wanted to make time with knowing I never would. I held on to the sheet with one hand. In the other hand was my cock.

I fucked a troll once.

"I swear to god I'll fucking strangle you right here mother-fucker! Where's our cd and cash?" I heard Beau yell.

Apparently he was pissed off. We were out one night and ran into this cat who engineered and promoted a show we played earlier one July at an art gallery in Point Pleasant, NJ. We, Buck, Beau and I were each supposed to get fifty bucks along with a mixed recording of our set. During negotiations we insisted on free booze as well, and so it was. It was now September.

The gallery was fantastically arranged. In the middle was a stage, with the people and displays circling all around it. All sorts of freaks and folks were there, mainly to lend support to Veronica Layne, the proud new owner of her first gallery on its opening night. She looked good. She was a high school friend of ours and quite insistent that we played her opening as she had seen us play before.

The band and I arrived early, around four o'clock in the afternoon. Beau had been awake for two days after swallowing a ridiculous amount of acid, blotters at that. Buck was steady Eddie man, ready to go. As for me, I stopped off to get some coke earlier that morning and was full blown maniacal by noon. The show was to start at seven so we had plenty of time to familiarize ourselves with the layout of the joint, carefully inspecting each hideaway corner we could duck off into a fire up a sweet bump. At this point we were using little jars filled with blow, each of us having our own you know, high class type shit.

Three other bands were playing; well really they weren't full bands just one guitar, one singer, one on the triangle type stuff. We were the only ones who needed the PA system. We were definitely the weirdoes of the bunch, slamming whiskey and beer while the other cats were sipping wine and casually doing a line or two.

We met Andy the promoter/engineer and immediately Beau didn't like him, hell, none of us did. A tall skinny prick with reddish long hair and a pair of sunglasses perched up on top of his head this dude, who we never met before that day had no idea what he was getting into I'm sure. He made the mistake of telling us to slow down on the booze. Poor bastard.

And the coke was flowing. I felt as if I could levitate and by the time we hit the stage an aura of light was holding the three of us together so beautifully, engulfing the stage and us as one being. The fucking drums were alive with soul and Beau looked like Hendrix when the hits of trips tied inside his bandana started to ooze their goodness.

After four songs Andy decided to lower the volume on us significantly much to the anger of the crowd. Oh shit, here we go again. Beau stopped playing as Buck and I were left in thought, knowing that an ass-kicking was on the horizon for this more than unfortunate cat. My hope was that we would all grab him and drag him outside as to not make an absolute mess of Veronica's new place. I was wrong.

Beau grabbed Andy by the throat and lifted him a few feet from the ground and then Buck came out of nowhere with a bottle of beer and hit the dangling fool in the stomach. That's right, the stomach! I've never seen such a sillier sight, as Andy's breath was completely taken away and he was grasping for air, sucking in like a fucking baby does on a teat. Rather than let him go and allow him to catch his breath Beau started continuously punching the suckling pig, from his face to his stomach and I for a second really thought Andy was going to drop and die right there on the floor.

It was my turn for a little fun so I grabbed the seemingly half dead man by his red hair and with it threw him into the drums causing all kinds of pieces to fly everywhere and paintings to fly off the walls onto the floor. The action stopped at this point and Veronica came over to display her disappointment and also brought a few of her friends, like seven of them to throw us out.

Hell, I couldn't argue man, we were douche bags for sure. When we got in my truck the laughter carried us for a few miles. I placed an order with the man and we rode off into the blue moonlit sky quite satisfied. We played well too man, definitely leaving the people wanting more; more music more action more everything.

So here's this unfortunate cocksucker who owes us money and a copy of the show that night with Colonel Van Bozwell screaming in his face at crowded bar on the Jersey Shore not knowing what was to happen, wearing a cold, someone just squeezed my balls kind of look on his face.

We were hammered, whiskey hammered to boot, and without cocaine for the first night in a great while. I stepped in between him and Beau in order to save all of us a beat down, seeing that Andy had many friends around, and don't you know the cocksucker paid us our cash and we followed him to his car to get the cd, which came out fabulously. He was actually a pretty cool cat.

After some more booze we decided to leave. Andy was outside smoking a cigarette by himself, directly in the path leading to my truck. As we approached him Beau lunged forward and kicked him straight in the dick.

"Next time it's for real man!" Beau said.

Wow we were assholes.

Her cunt it spoke in rhymes, long beautiful nasty rhymes. She was the girl who everyone slept with, and for a gram of coke you could have as well.

Very short, around five foot one Jill was, drop dead gorgeous, the kind of girl you would marry had she not been such a terrible whore. I mean as far as whores go she was not your textbook one. She worked for a fashion designer in New York City five days a week and was really making quite a life for herself.

The weekends however told quite different tale indeed.

My buddy Les introduced me to her at a party one winter night in a cozy little restaurant bar in Hoboken, NJ. A shot of booze and a line and I spent the night with her in a Hotel a few blocks down from the bar.

She was freaky man. We were all over that fucking room snorting lines and drinking beers throughout the night. My buddy Buck told me the story about Stevie Nicks, the one where she had paid a gal to go on tour with her back in the seventies with her sole job being to blow cocaine up ole' Stevie's ass whenever she requested. Suddenly I had a thought.

"Hey Jill how'd you like me to blow some coke up your ass with this here straw?"

"Please do," she replied.

So I filled the straw with coke and blew it up her ass. She enjoyed it, so I did it again a bit later.

We woke up late that afternoon both quite satisfied regarding our time together. Few words were spoken; I believe I said thank-you. We walked through the merry-go-round door of the hotel and hit the street. I made a left. She didn't.

In the summer of 1992 I was at the pinnacle of my psychedelic career, tripping out at least three days a week with whoever the hell would come aboard the terrific ride. My buddy Jody was the fortunate soul who climbed on one super sunny muggy night one summer in July.

Jody worked with this fanatical coke head named Lenny at a sub shop. At this point I was still afraid of cocaine and it kind of went against the tripping balls scene if you get me. Anyhow this cracked out cat's parents were filthy rich and they were away for a month or so on holiday, leaving their son alone in their ridiculously large home which bode well for anyone who had a sack of blow or anything else imaginable.

Jody and I scored some green skull hits from a lunatic who worked at a hospital who would trip every other day while working. Fucking crazy man. Lenny extended the invitation to us and we latched onto it like thieves in the night to whatever lies in wait. Jody explained the layout of the house to me which included a basement certainly designed by a balls out kind of junk head, with a professional style pool table along with a ping pong table, knock hockey, super chexx hockey, poker table, extensive video game selection, projection television, and all sorts of other games we could get into while in our glory flying high on acid.

Yeah, I'll go

Reliving the scene now as a fellow cocaine adorer reveals the absolute playground scene we walked into when we got there. A giant mirror table, I mean ten fit comfortably, centered the pristine living room which had cathedral ceilings and was roughly eight hundred square feet. Grand windows let in the bright pale moon around the tied back golden curtains. A full bar with a dozen seats completed the serene scene serene especially to the full blown degenerates who entered the house fit for royalty.

It's hard to imagine anyone being out of place at junk house but at the far end of the table, seat number nine, sat a tall long hair tucked under a John Deere cap dude wearing overalls and filthy brown boots covered in green paint named Dave. He wasn't snorting any blow, which was immediately obvious as he was peaceful and calm lounging back in the black soft as a cloud chair that engulfed him.

Jody and I dropped our hits an hour before arriving and I was tripping pretty good by the time we got there. In my paranoid state I didn't say a word to anyone except Jody ordering him to hurry us to the basement so I could get back to peace. And so we went.

Jody and I played a lot of pool during this time so the first thing we did was start a game of straight pool to a thousand which, had we finished would have lasted at least twenty hours. We fancied ourselves great players but in fact we had no business playing straight pool where you had to call every shot including the break, playing safeties and all that kind of shit, but, we started playing nonetheless.

After an hour or so I was feeling fantastic. We decided to take a trek upstairs and dig on the scene for a while, studying the faces of the folks up there as they melted away slowly to us. My attention was focused on Dave who was still sitting in his cozy chair oblivious to the racket going on around him. I grabbed a vacant seat to his left and introduced myself.

As we sat exchanging pointless words for a while he reached for his back pack at his feet, pulled out a ginormous sack of weed, pinched of a hunk and grabbed a pack of rolling papers from his shirt pocket, all in a relaxed state you would expect from a man of his demeanor, you know, all business.

I sat in awe watching him as in only sixty seconds he rolled the most perfect joint without setting the wrap on the table once, doing it all in his hands with his long skinny fingers like a surgeon opening up a heart. He licked it closed like a grandfather bullfrog snatching bugs and popped it in his mouth while pulling a pack of matches from his other shirt pocket.

Who lights joints with matches? Hell, who wears fucking overalls?

Jody and I sat upstairs for an hour in a trance, watching Dave roll and light three more joints smoking them like cigarettes. One of the chicks snorting blow asked him for a pull and he refused her quickly. He did, however swiftly roll one up for her, as apparently he didn't share his own with anyone, but was more than happy to twist you up one for yourself.

Just as Jody, Dave, and I began to have an actual conversation Lenny collapsed to the floor appearing to be having a heart attack. Man you never saw people get up and run out of a house so damn fast. I looked at Jody in a "what the fuck are we going to do kind of way" and he reciprocated it right back at me. We then looked to Dave.

He was calmly rolling up another bone. As he finished it he struck a match and the trails which came off it blew my fucking marbles man.

"Eddie, call 911. Jody, go downstairs and turn off the lights. When you guys are done grab your stuff and go home," Dave instructed, in a soft spoken yet quite firm way.

"What are you gonna do man?" I asked.

"I'm going to finish smoking this bone, roll out of here and head on back to Seattle. This place brings me down man," replied Dave.

And we all left.

During the next week at work Jody learned that Lenny had a heart attack the night we were there and died shortly after the ambulance arrived. A casualty of the scene indeed a shame it was. Shit happens.

Annihilated on a summer night at a two beer for two bucks joint I found myself in quite the situation. Anything I said to the ladies that night was like poetry, at least in my mind. I'm sure if I just "hey, wanna fuck?" I'd have landed one in the sack anyway, but man, a pack of six chicks surrounded my three friends and me and inevitably we all wound up at the beach house they rented for the summer, drunk as fuck and ready to hump. It's funny how cheap beers brings out the big shot in all of us you know?

Between the six girls there were two three packs of sisters, with one pack cousins to the other, a family affair you see. Initially I was sweet on Christi, having kissed her drunkenly back at the bar for a bit but as I awaited her arrival into the bedroom her cousin Barbara entered instead. Christi was short 'bout five two and super sexy, with nice thick lips and long blonde wavy hair, a peach.

Barb, not so much. She wasn't ugly by any stretch, in fact in her own way, five and half feet or so with short jet black hair and ridiculously huge tits that complimented her golden delicious ass so well she was indeed a runner up, but not so distantly, so, I figured okay, why not, what's the fucking difference anyhow?

As strange as our relationship commenced the strangeness only heightened for the rest of that summer. For starters she likey the cocaine too. When I woke up that morning she greeted me with a glass straw and a heap of fantastic shit. Ordinarily I prefer using a dollar bill but Jesus Christ it was one hell of a wake up call.

We strolled down to beach and sat at a beach side bar for the afternoon, making more than a thousand or so trips to the bathroom for replenishment bumps. We went back to her place and everyone was gone. The cocaine was also gone so I asked her how we could get more immediately. She had the answer I craved: my neighbor a few houses down has it. Let's go.

Up to the house we went and an older cat named Marty let us in, leading us right to the table containing as much coke as you could handle all about it. He carved out giant rattlesnake lines for the next few hours, without any request for cash, in fact I offered him a fifty and he insistently refused as if my cash was infected with syphilis.

This guy was unreal man. He had long salt and pepper hair with an equally zebra like beard, quite long as well. Wire thin silver framed circular glasses exuded a real artsy vibe from his face while his eyes radiated wealth. I felt extremely awkward about not paying for anything but that left me after a few more lines when I realized he was just another fuck up like me whose shit stank like shit and blood bled crimson maroon as all of ours do and whose throat I'd cut ear to ear if I had to.

Barb was yapping up a storm like she was in a hair salon, which is exactly where she worked. During a brief four seconds of silence I hunched over to do a line while Marty so matter-of-factly asked Barb, "So I gather you guys fucked last night?"

I started laughing immediately and the breath which catapulted from toes and out my mouth blew at least two ounces of coke all over the floor leaving floating flakes in its wake. How I wished I could beam myself the fuck out of there. I furiously apologized over and again until the calmness in Barb's and Marty's faces paralyzed my tongue.

Finally Marty jumped up and said, "It's alright man, I'll just go get some more."

"What do you mean it's alright man, are you fucking ignorant? I just dumped two grand all over the floor and it's *cool* with you? You're fucking mad man! Barb, is this guy for real?" I shouted.

The two of them got up and told me to follow them into one of the bedrooms so I did. Marty swung the door open and I had a flashback to my high school days in physics class. Beakers and test tubes were scattered all about the laboratory like scene. He had fucking Bunsen burners man! I love Bunsen burners. Marty spoke again.

"It's cool because I make the stuff Eddie. I'm a chemist. Coke costs me virtually nothing to make. You can have whatever the hell you can handle for free so long as you take care of Barb. She's like a daughter to me man so treat her well."

"Okay captain," I thought.

This was unbelievable. I now had the ability to run rampant all over the fucking bars with free blow and all that was required was that I fuck a chick that basically did whatever the hell
I said.

96

"Yeah, I'll take good care of her man."

A week later Barb's parents wanted to meet me so they invited us out on their sailboat one Saturday afternoon out of Sandy Hook. It all sounded great. The wind was gusting when we arrived so, with a twelve pack of Heinekens in hand and having just snorted enough coke so my nose almost bled but didn't, Barb and I walked hand in hand down the dock and boarded the twenty something foot clipper.

After the initial introductions her pop wasted no time in putting me to work. I had not a glimpse of an idea what he was telling me to do but shit I was riled up and moving four hundred miles a second and goddamn it I was a fucking sailor man! The wind hit our sails perfectly. The white clouds above were spread out enough so the sun shone brightly uninterrupted.

Barb stripped down to her bikini and laid out on the bow looking extraordinarily fine. Her mom was quiet but super friendly, passing me beers like a bartender at happy hour just as soon as I finished them. We dropped anchor after thirty smooth sailing minutes and Barb and I jumped in the bay and lay cozily on a raft her mother made sure to remember to bring. And for an hour and a half my world was right.

We jumped back on the boat and it all hit the shitter right quick: Her old man was slowly sipping away my last beer and the last remnants of blow in my nose were long gone. What's worse was we had fifty miles ahead of us to get back to the marina and the goddamn wind died and the stubborn old prick refused to turn the fucking engine on. I shot Barb a look of "are you fucking kidding me?" and in return she shrugged her shoulders. It was torture knowing that in her car a thick bag of space blow was waiting for me to inhale it. Blow wind. Blow goddamn it!

Twouldn't. For two more hours the old man of the sea waited but it never came. I was ready to start killing everyone and taking over the damn ship when at last the ever so cock-sucking fuck cranked the engine and we were off. I knew Barb and I were not long for each other after that day. My dilemma was without her I'd have to start paying for blow again. I hung on for a bit longer. Damn that stuff had me by the balls.

One morning we awoke early as Barb had to go up north to work. Apparently the night before I agreed to drive her car up and stay at her parent's place until she got off. Her folks were out of town so it wasn't the end of the world. Marty packed us up a jumbo bag of coke with an afternoon's supply because he was flying to San Diego for some kind of who the fuck cares convention for the morning and coming right back.

We got to her work and of course I had to meet her co-workers. I hate that kind of shit. Everyone's all phony and what not, including myself, when in reality I would have gone out of my way to bring misery and pain to each and every mother-fucker in the place bringing them down into my chaotic mess.

With Barb at work and a sack of blow I drove off to her parent's house in Clark, NJ about thirty minutes from the salon agreeing to pick her up at six.

Inside I immediately began sneezing and my eyes began to swell. And then the fucking cat appeared, black, fat, and a real quick sucker. For the next eight hours I had to fight him off as he would lunge and scratch the hell out of me. He was too damn quick for me to grab despite all of the cocaine running through my body. It was complete madness. I chased that fucker through the house all day and incurred ridiculous claw marks all over my face and body.

At five o'clock I cornered that cocksucker and he must have run out of juice because he just sat there. I ran at him and still he didn't move. With all the power I had and all of the misery he caused me that day exploding in my mind I kicked that sucker square in the stomach and he flew directly into wall falling helplessly to the ground. I grabbed a smoke and sat down for one more line before leaving to pick up Barb. He didn't move.

We left her work and headed right back down to the beach house. Straight into Marty's we went where two extremely generous fantastic super terrifical lines were on the table as per our request over the phone on the way down. Barb went down on the line like a hungry whore as I finished all the blow we had and she was without for some time. Marty sat there in silence tired from a red eye flight he returned on just an our or so before.

I snorted up my line and suddenly realized it would be the last taste of alien coke I'd ever have, and I was okay with it. I stood up.

"Marty, thanks for being a genuinely nice dude. Barb, I had a good time with you this summer but goddamn I've had enough. By the way, I killed your cat. He's dead on your kitchen floor."

No responses no nothing. I walked from the house one contented son-of-a-bitch. I think about that summer from time to time almost missing it. The coke that is.

VI. <u>Tropicalia</u>

Upon entering the doors of this fine establishment, a thirty bed upscale tanning salon down the Jersey Shore, I felt an uncontrollable bliss, as if being stroked off by a goddess, while the devil himself shook my hand insuring countless dark days in store. I was home.

My best childhood friend, Tony, and his family were the pioneers for mega tanning salons, giants of the industry. At this point in my life, I was on the path to nowhere and was getting there quickly. Tony was the day to day manager of the store and was also the new proud owner of his own. I didn't know it at the time, but he hired me to be his replacement and groomed me right from the get.

A bit of background for those who've never been to, worked in, or had any other knowledge of the goings on in tanning salons: of course the predominant attraction to someone like myself, a 22 year old kid, was the ridiculous amounts of good looking broads who rolled in and out of the joint wearing lets say, basically not much, seeking advice on everything from how to tan their asses to where the fuck's the party and all in between, good and bad. Like a magician I'd send them into little rooms, they'd get naked, and for ten to fifteen minutes they'd lie in a bed and come out looking immensely better giving me all the praise. My ego was immeasurable most days.

Don't get me wrong however. For every genuine hottie that pranced in I'd have to endure roughly three not so nice ones, knowing of course that they'd be getting undressed as well (I gag as I write and remember a particularly plump chick calling me over to her room requesting me to put lotion on her back, a request quickly denied of course). I mean shit, if you're a 250 plus chick, would you rather tan at the beach, with everyone throwing bologna at you, or locked up in a room alone knowing no one can possibly see the tremendously thick sacks of lard burned into your varicose ass, or the caverns left by the rivet gun old pineapple face Noriega endorsed from way back, which has left your flap- jacked titties resembling a fine dish of scrambled eggs Grandma Schiavone made me as a kid.?

As this image I've painted resonates into your medulla I will not pretend that I've never taken a couple of these, not so hounded hounds down town, you dig? It gets real hot and muggy in August in New Jersey, and sometimes the last customer of the night will do no matter what, (well, almost) especially after a few fists full of cocaine has rendered your ability to differentiate acceptable behaviors from well, insanity.

Indeed, I've seen all kinds of nauseating horrific shit, but the payoff was tremendous. If you can't get laid running a tanning salon, kindly chop off your cock and pass it to me, so I can screw 'em twice at once for fuck's sake. I mean hell, shootin fish in a barrel you know. Good times they were.

Alright back to it. There were two bathrooms in the joint. The customer's was fine in its own right, small but cozy, with almost perfect lighting. The sink was at a height which made it possible to chop a few without feeling like a you were in a dollhouse, with enough room left and right of the handles that fit any desired amount of blow both in width and length. I do recall my customers, at least the snorters describing their experience in there to be "just like home", which made me feel rather nice I must say. I always made sure to keep it clean in there, for the greater good you see.

Most of my engagements with the powder took place in the office toilet, although for fucks and kisses I would use the customer's for a change-up once and again.

Before describing this Camelot type of setting I will tell you, before beginning work at The Tropicalia, I was a casual cocaine abuser. I recall at one time being tremendously afraid of it, while I was dropping acid at least twice a week and thinking you guys are fucked up snorting that shit. The economics didn't jive either. I mean forty a gram for forty minutes or two blotters for five each or three for ten man for twenty hours. I fancy myself quite a mathematical genius you see.

Inevitably all rational thinking left as I took my first stroll into the office of the trop and was quickly embraced by the ambiance which massaged my spine. Of course I wasn't sure at the time what it was all about but I knew damn well some great shit would be going down in there. The fold out couch on the wall shed a bit of light.

On the left as you walk in, a long black desk hugged the wall. Above it, shelves held stacks of paperwork and assorted what nots. In the left corner mounted on a movable television stand sat a fifteen inch monitor which, when turned on, provided a perfect view of the front of the store focusing mainly on the desk where the computer and register sat. Many a time, probably in the thousands, that monitor afforded me the pleasure of snorting in relative peace, although after getting tweaked my paranoia would set in and during the day shadows of people walking by the outside of the storefront looked like people to me standing at the counter.

The couch was straight ahead, brown and inviting. Miscellaneous tanned up queens were postured on all the walls and a big white lotion cabinet was on the immediate right as you entered. Oh shit, we had a fucking freezer in the back left corner containing pretzels and ice cream, stuff we would sell once in a while. Once in a *long* while. Considering who I worked for, let's just say if a sawed off arm with no fingers was in there I was prepared to handle it.

Back behind the lotion cabinet and on the right was the bathroom. The set up was the same as the other one except a stand-up shower provided relief for those long nights, or days for that matter. The angle from the toilet, with the door opened was a perfect shot right to the monitor, maximizing the ability to get about the business at hand. I'm quite certain for a fact, and I mean this true, the designer of the salon who I knew well, had the interests of cocaine in mind during construction.

The one disadvantage of doing lines in the office bathroom was that Sonny, the owner, always parked around back and would come in through the back door, leaving me no warning as to his arrival.

One particular day I just finished a monster line and as I left the bathroom my nose was bleeding a bit as he entered. He knew what was up, but for reasons I still don't fully understand he never confronted me on the issue. I did feel like the douche bag that I was when he would come in and find me fucked up, but only until he left. After that it was right back at it, naturally, without a thought of any repercussion. It was as if when he came in and I was all balls out fucked up he would only stay a short while, then leave allowing me to continue on. Christ, he lived only ten minutes from the store for fuck's sake.

It was during my first summer working at the Trop that I was reacquainted with my best childhood friend Joe Carpini. He, Tony, and I raised a tremendous amount of hell growing up. They once held down Joe's older brother Tony as I proceeded to whack the shit out of him with a tennis racket. You know, the usual ten year old stuff.

I hadn't seen him in a few years as he was living on his parents' seventy acre farm in the middle of where the fuck am I Ohio. He was back in town and was looking to start a blues band. Joe is without question one of the most insanely talented guitarist I've known. When we were fourteen he told Tony and he was punished for the entire summer. Come September, cat came out of his basement sounding like a fifty year seasoned Delta bluesman. His problem was he had no fire in his ass, and no matter how much I tried lighting one it was all in vain.

We set up a jam at Joe's place in historic Belmar New Jersey, about two blocks from cocaine central near the beach. Mitch Grippaldi or Grippopotamous as we knew him would also be there. He played a steady Eddie rhythm guitar which could not be thought of as anything other than cash.

I arrived on a Saturday around noon with a case of Heineken and my beautiful bass on my back eager to finally play some good ole' blues with the boys. Before beginning we slammed down some beers with whiskey chasers, and sucked down big fat bone Grippo so eloquently twisted up. Stumbling over Joe's pit bull Harley, I made it downstairs to the basement and we started to play.

We stumbled on to some deep hammering down blues get up and shit and hell I was struggling to keep up. It would go smooth for about a minute then I had to stop due to the cramps causing my fingers to lock up like some retarded freak coming off some black tar heroin. After the third stop I screamed out, "Alright mother-fuckers, if you want me to play like that you'd better get some blow delivered here right now!"

Thirty minutes later, the man who would become my dealer for the Trop arrived and laid a rich man's chunk of blow on the table, smashed it in the bag, then carved out four most certainly much more than generous bulk lines of the purest cocaine I had snorted up until that point in my life.

Jamie, the Fat Man as we called him, and he was a fat mother-fucker, had been hooking up Joe for a while. He was about six foot, two seventy-five, with a dumb ass look on his face which reminded me of Potsie from Happy Days. Through our conversation I learned that he lived about five minutes from my house, which was also five minutes from the Trop, which meant I was to begin my full blown coke career come Monday morning at work.

Oh yeah, the jam went well from that point on.

So next day Sunday came and I drove to the fat man's house for a sack of goods. The door opened and holy hell the blow queen of Brick High School, Justine herself stood before me. This broad was disgusting. She actually looked like the fat man, with a more neatly attended to chin on the back of her head. In high school I met her at a party and she did her business on my boys. Wow was I fucked up. Afterwards she gave me her number and told me to call her the next time I was drunk and she would pick me up, suck me off, and then drive me home. So I did. More than a couple few several weekly daily Sundays Tuesdays and long cold winter nights. Needless to say the look of horror on her face was expected as she opened the door and let me in. She begged me not to tell her husband, the fat man, with a pleading tone as if I had been seeking her the last eight years, perhaps not realizing she was not exactly my fondest or proudest accomplishment of my early "I'll fuck a snake if you hold it" days.

Just then the fat man came into view at the top of the stairs which was immediately on the left as you entered the house, and I realized how perfect they were for each other.

Good for them, poor bastards.

I climbed the stairs and followed him into the business room, quite spectacular I must say. Apparently blow queen Justine kept a tidy home. On a large table sat a butcher's scale with an ass load of coke on it, with its sweet aroma tickling every nerve in my face. The fat man chopped two canons, and once again I realized what a fantastic connection I made. I believe I paid a hunge and half for an eight-ball, but naturally I was in no rush to leave due to the free tastes to come. Now, I'm definitely one of those mother-fuckers who runs his mouth constantly after a few lines, but this cat was too much man. It was obvious old boy didn't have many friends, because the shit he was laying on me had been building for quite some time. He was telling about what a cunt his wife was and about at that point I had to hit the high road. Damn if he only knew how many dicks his wife swallowed before he came along. The sheer horror..

Neither before nor since have I met a coke junk head who was a fat fuck.

I was up all night firing down lines drinking booze and playing cards. At eight o'clock I took a shower, had breakfast, consisting of four mentholated smokes and headed to work.

And there she waited, fifteen minutes before we opened, sucking down a sausage egg and cheese: Leslie Fitch, the daily tanner, the reason why people feel tanning is not good for you. I mean truth be told, a bit of ultraviolet rays are without a doubt *good* for you. This chick looked like a fucking alligator, and an old one at that.

"Hey Leslie, bear with me, I haven't slept at all." Leslie and I were actually pretty good pals, even though she was a dike, and not a good looking one. She talks like, looks like, and acts like Marge Simpson's sisters, right down to the cancer cough and all. Her partner was no looker either, and when they were together at the salon I couldn't stand it for more than a smoke. In fact those two were probably the reason I started smoking my cigs so damn fast, you know, to get the hell away from them as the three of us usually had a smoke outside when they would come by.

Leslie quickly knew what I was all about, having seen me every morning for a couple of months in the throws of ridiculous cocaine morning blues, reeking of whiskey. Apparently she also had a sweet tooth for powder and that morning she asked me if I could hook her up.

"Yes," I said.

She explained that it had been years since she last had some, and was suddenly in the mood, claiming to see how much fun I was having, which to me was impossible because I only saw her first thing in the morning after snorting *all my shit* and realistically I would have cut someone's throat if they had a line.

In any event, I told her to bring me some cash later that morning and I'd take care of her early in the afternoon. She then laid some blue and yellow capsules on me and said they would help me sleep. (Turns out they caused my jaw to lock up for a few hours but, eventually I did get some rest). She gave me three hundred dollars without inquiring what she would be getting for it. The wheel in my coke infested mind began to race: my thieving, lying, incredibly selfish, maniacal mind.

Immediately I called the fat man and told him I needed shit as soon as yesterday. He agreed to swing by and get the cash, then ride up to Asbury Park to see his man. I figured I could easily swindle about half of what three bills would get, roughly two eight-balls. And I was correct.

Leslie had no goddamn clue about what coke went for those days. I had the fat man split the rock right down the middle, two bags. When Leslie came back to pick hers up I handed one to her in perhaps the shadiest fucking drug deal ever. I was talking with a little honey when Leslie walked in. I gave her the bug eye to let her know I would be with her in a minute. The chick I was talking to just wouldn't shut up so Leslie interrupted and told me she needed to speak with me outside.

I excused myself and we walked out front. I quickly passed her a sack and went back inside to find the girl I was talking to with her jaw on the goddamn floor having witnessed the whole passing of the goods. Oh well, fuck her, she wouldn't have lasted two days with me anyhow, the little prissy bitch.

For the rest of that day I was fucking crazy wearing off the tile in the path that led to and fro the office, being real deliberate in my actions, quick as a cat man. At times I recall various people commenting on how goddamn wired I was almost smelling the coke oozing from my nose. Man I felt great.

After work, I had about a gram and one sixty-fourth left, and I proceeded to Foster's liquor store where Uncle Charlie was waiting because he had some Cubans for me. Charlie owned the joint, and for some reason he always liked me, probably due to the fact I bought a twelve back every day from his store for the previous five years. I mean hell, no need to go anywhere else. Coldest beer in towns you know.

I followed Uncle Chuck into his office and he laid down three Romeo and Juliet, Romulus and Reamus as we called them, and I passed him sixty bucks. We spoke of the Yankees and I assured him we'd win the whole fucking thing again as I did every year. He was a doubter, nervous you know. He was also a gambler and every once in a while when he was struggling I'd throw him a winner to get him back in the red, or black, however the hell that goes. I was always able to pick winners for everyone else, but holy Christ the second I threw down my own cash you could guarantee a blowout the other way. Anyhow, Charlie and I shook hands and parted. Twelve Heinekens in hand I walked out of the store feeling like the king of the known world, and the unknown world for that matter. I figured I'd better get another gram of powder to get me through the night. And so I did.

Queen Justine herself answered the door looking as disgusting as ever. I nodded then raced upstairs. Fat man threw me a jewel wrapped up in a little foil, we snorted a couple cannons and I got the fuck out of there.

Back at my house, well Tony's house, the house I lived in, we had a full crowd. I used to look at them with great anticipation for good times. Now however, all I could see were poor mother-fuckers who would be nagging the shit out of me for "one" line. Anyone who toured on the cocaine circuit knows if you pass a line to someone you essentially were giving away half of whatever you had.

To my surprise however, everyone had their own sack, most with a gram some halfsies on an eight ball. Nice. Man the shit started flying right off the bat. The Madden brothers, Jeff, Doug, and David, were getting into it about their old man. Peter Madden was a Vietnam vet, a decorated one at that. He had the most kills in his unit, hope that's the right word, and was one crazy mofo often having distinct flashbacks reciting exact orders he gave back in the war.

Apparently before the Madden boys came by that night, Old Pete was in rare form, going into explicit details regarding a mission where he had to slaughter entire families because a sniper Gook was hiding out amongst them, picking off Americans as he hid from village to village, a real prick.

David, the quietest of the three, was sitting on the couch Indian style smoking a joint as Jeff vacuumed up a huge line into his snout, which was quite large I must say. He could probably store an ounce of coke up there with no one being the wiser. Doug was getting fired up one because he was next to sniff, two because Jeff was loudly expressing his displeasure of his father bringing up some crazy shit from the past.

Doug went down for his line like a jailed pussy eater would upon his release. As he came up, with powder falling from his nose and all over his face, he screamed. "You've never smelled death Jeffrey so shut the fuck up! You don't know what it's like!"

We all started cracking up. Tony, who was rolling up a coke centered joint knocked over his beer. Doug used to be a grave digger and apparently felt he was on an even plain with anyone and everyone who's ever stabbed, maimed, tortured, hacked-up, or pushed someone through a wood chipper the ignorant bastard. He told us stories before about times he and his co-workers dug up bodies. Now, shitty and traumatic as that may have been these already dead fuckers he dug up were, well, already goddamn dead!

Man I loved those Madden boys though. Quick as shit to fight for you, and extremely loyal in all other ways, backing my play no matter what several times, saving my ass on a few occasions.

The rest of the evening was filled with countless tales of women we never screwed, situations which never occurred, and all the other kind of nonsense we could muster up. About three a.m. I remembered I had a couple valium lying around and I figured I should get a couple winks in before work.

Waking up or coming to I should say was actually great. Somehow I saved two rather thick lines for breakfast. Got to have a well balanced meal you know so I poured a nice glass of whiskey and threw the coke in there. The coke would get me going and the booze would take the edge off a bit. Smooth. Good morning mother-fuckers!

I made it to work right at nine and sure as shit Leslie the dike was waiting there for me. Damn she looked terrible, I mean more than usual, which I though impossible.

"You alright kid?" I asked her.

She nodded in the affirmative and asked me when I could get her more coke and as quick as I said now she pulled out three hundred bucks like Doc Holliday drawing on some poor bastard trying to cheat him in poker.

"Well, alright then Leslie, you know the deal, I'll call you when we're all set," I told her. It was at this point she said something that still puzzles me to this day.

"You know, if I was ten years younger Eddie."

What in the name of Rasputin was she fucking meaning there? If she was ten years younger what, would she fuck a goat, would she eat my ass, what the fuck, you're a *butch* you cunt-eating dildo plunging pig, were you going to be swayed by me, a person who wouldn't lick your box for immortality?

Thanks for the cash Leslie. I'll call you in a bit. Man, she must have licked some bad pussy the night before, as her breath spoke volumes on the matter.

I got the fat man on the phone and briefed him on the situation.

"She's an animal!" he spewed.

Yeah man, now get dressed come get the cash and go see your man. Split the shit in two bags with one a bit heavier than the other, get it?

And it was in motion.

This pattern continued on for several months. Nine o'clock get cash from the animal, call the fat man, and get a free eight ball. Even my boys at the liquor store started playing ball with me. Every evening after work, two packs of smokes twelve pack of Heineys and a small bottle of bourbon whiskey, five bucks. I had all I could have asked for: A four hundred a day addiction for five dollars. Right on.

I stumbled into the liquor store one day and the cat behind the counter who didn't even know me but gave me free booze asked me if I bought Cubans from Uncle Charlie. When I said yes he started shaking his head, as if he was my father and found out I got my third DWI. He told me they were fake, Dominicans not Cubans. Man I was pissed. That dirty scum bag was ripping me off! Uncle Charlie my ass.

Then it all made sense. Hell, I was robbing him blind every day for booze. The least I could do was pay twenty for a five dollar cigar every two weeks. I kept my end of the charade up for quite a while, passing him sixty for three fraudulent stogies. I also began bringing up a case of beer and the good shit, Glen Fitich to the counter with me. Screw me and I'm gonna fuck your whole family. I'm gonna dig up your grandmother with Doug Madden and fuck every space between her bones and then shit in her grave. I'm gonna wait eight years until your ten year old daughter graduates high school and fuck her like some maniacal prisoner would and then throw her on your lawn you degenerate cocksucker!

Ah Betty Tobler. Hot little number who came in Monday Wednesday Friday to tan up her fine little ass. She'd pull up in her silver Volvo with a twenty ounce coffee from 7-11 for me around ten am like clockwork. Standing five foot one on her best day, thirty-two years lived, with straight, long, jet black hair which she loved to have pulled from behind, she was it.

I'd be all fucked up flying off the walls when she would come in and apparently she was quite intrigued by my tales of cocaine, rock n' roll, and other random acts of debauchery, as was I with her seemingly innocent ways.

After she left one day I went in to clean the tanning bed she lied in and found her black laced thong panties sitting on the chair. You dirty whore, now I really wanted to get on her. We flirted all the time but I thought she was just playing around. Ten minutes later she called me and asked if I got the surprise she left me. She then told me to take her out that Friday night and show her some fun. Um, sure.

She picked me up in her silver Volvo wearing a perfect black sort of sun dress. You know, the guy who invented the sun dress deserves life long free blow-jobs from whoever the fuck he wants upon demand. In fact he should be able just to point at a girl and not say a word. Point to her, then his cock, and without hesitation she should prance over, unzip him, and start sucking, that fucking genius.

I decided we would go up to Downtown House in beautiful Red Bank, New Jersey. There was always a great blues/funk band there on Friday nights, and on most occasions the chicks were dressed to screw you know.

We went upstairs and she followed me into the bathroom to snort a few. A one manner it was with a lock, a rarity indeed. She informed me she never did blow and asked if she was going to enjoy it. With a smile of disbelief I assured her she would. Holy fuck she snorted like a champ, a seasoned veteran, a fucking aardvark man! Take me home and fuck me she said, as I bounced her beautiful ass off the four walls holding us from destroying the whole damn layout of the place. Thing was, I was twenty two, I lived with my parents, in a rather small place, with the only bathroom located directly next to the wall where my bed was, but hell, when a chick tells you to fuck her, you fuck her.

"Let's go," I said.

We sped home and hell, wasted no time. About thirty minutes into it, at least that's the time I'm going with, was probably more like seven, she said the words Mr. Joseph Edwin Krakelberg the third told me about: Put it in the other one! Christ she told me to pull it up a notch and stick it in her ass! Joe screwed a thirty plus gal a few months earlier, and his experience was the same as mine. He said all women over thirty demanded it in the number two hole, practically begged for it. His theory was correct.

After meeting her demand let's say I was finished in a minute, quicker than getting the rush from the first line of coke of the evening. Before I could get my cigarette lit she said calmly, matter-of-factly, like she was answering a trigonometry problem, "Oh yeah, I'm married, is that going to be a problem for you?"

Now, it's hard to get pissed off at someone who just let you perform an act on her which is illegal in many states, but shit, I couldn't help like feeling I was going to hell at that very moment, and not to use my front row tickets I held for Jimi Hendrix, to get sodomized myself by the good old Devil himself.

"No, that's okay for me Betty," I said with a smile still shaking from the dirty deed.

I proceeded to meet her every other weekend for the next several months. She began to speak of leaving her husband, an emergency room doctor, with the expectation that she and I, along with her two kids, would start a new life together. I told her if she did I would move in with her husband so I could be the doctor's wife, and enjoy an unlimited supply of loot with a beachfront home and an amazing boat. What a twisted bird man, where was her brain? Hell, I was twenty two so I had sort of an excuse for the adultery, I was the merely the stick she was sitting on, if not me, someone would have done it, you know?

I continued to see her for the next few weeks. One morning after doing a tremendous line I was out front sucking down a mentholated piece of heaven when a silver Volvo came screaming around the back of the store towards me. Fuck. I went inside to grab the equalizer, a giant black mag-lite flashlight and started loosening up with it to get ready to smash her husband's skull in before he could kill me.

Son-of-a-bitch, it was Pat Bartolli, a good friend of mine, a cat who always gave me tips on the ponies and who knew about my deal with Betty because well, I told him. He had the same damn car and figured one, he'd fuck with me, and two I'd be riled up on the blow and was sure to react like the cokehead I was.

"Hey, in the sixth today at Monmouth Park there's a horse named Quackerbarrow. He should be going off around twelve to one. Lay some cash down on him," he said, without mention or hinting or acknowledging the fact he just caused half a shit to pop from my ass.

"Bed two Pat, thanks for the tip, you cocksucker," I halfheartedly said to him.

Quackerbarrow went off at fifteen to one and with a hundred on him I took fifteen hundred.

I decided at this point the Betty Tobler train needed to hit a brick wall quickly so I called her and told her I needed to speak to her about redefining the nature of our relationship. She told me to meet her at Martell's Tiki Bar that evening.

When I got there she was wearing a bikini top and tight ass little shorts and was sucking down an enormous margarita. I came right out with it telling her I was finished with all this shit between us. I explained about the mess in my shorts from the morning. I went on to tell her how fucked up I thought she was for screwing up her home, especially her kids, for they had met me once at a coincidental meeting at the beach and she introduced us. Why in the hell would you think I, a young man with much left to conquer, would even consider settling down with a ready made goddamn family? Have you lost your marbles lady?

"Just fuck me one more time and I'll leave you alone," she responded.

So I did, and then true to her word I never even saw her again, not even at the salon. I kind of missed her.

The split came just in time. The cocaine scene in town was beginning to blow up and the fat man started dealing with a new supplier who had better shit, better prices, and better hours. My mind was now clear, well clearer, and I had to focus my attention on getting new clients, which wasn't hard because everyone knew my story.

I'll tell you man, if I was not such a degenerate junkie I could have banked some serious cabbage. I was moving three to four ounces of blow a week, but instead of selling the free ounce I was getting, not any of it, I was like a damn king, living on blow, coffee, beer, pills, ice pops, jolly ranchers and whiskey. High class you see.

Relationships with chicks consisted taking a hostage a day and filling her up with drugs, booze, and myself. I hardly saw my parents either. I usually went to their house a few times a week to eat but man I couldn't eat anything, which didn't bode well for my diabetes so much. Candy and ice pops kept me from collapsing and dying from low blood sugars. My doctor, who I was almost completely honest with, assured me only a couple more years on this planet, but it didn't matter much to me. I couldn't stop, I wouldn't stop, and I didn't want to stop. To me I was living the dream and all who were trying to get me to change were the enemy.

The only person I actually stopped to consider how much I was fucking up was my ten year younger brother Jethro. Man he's seen me at my absolute worst. I remember one time he rode his bike over to my house. It was ten in the morning and he wanted to play some basketball. I went to the bathroom and snorted three lightning bolted lines and came out ready to go. He had a look of horror in his face and when I asked him what the fuck was wrong he started wiping his nose while his eyes were popping out of his head to signal to me I had shit on my nose and face. When I went into the bathroom and saw myself in the mirror my nose was bleeding with most of it engulfed with coke. He went home. He didn't tell my parents anything either. He kept it inside and surely battled with it for a time. In fact he told me how much he struggled growing up as my little bro when I made my amends to him.

I love that boy.

But wow how mother-fuckers love that cocaine! I had the perfect cover working at the tanning salon. One session with a pack of lotion, that's eighty bucks you fuck. And screw fronting people. I didn't go for that shit man. I fucked over many dealers before on that deal so I knew about the absolute fucking havoc it caused. Madness even.

Through strict dealing efforts my efforts were slick. Most of the time there were groups of friends who would each want a sack of their own to go out and party with. I would sell just the hot shot of the bunch one giant bag and have him divvy it up between his douche-bag friends, allowing him to split any way he chose with his take being heavy.

One particular scoundrel comes to mind as far as being a real pain in the ass: Dan Henley. He drove a heavy duty built for speed mustang, a blue one, and he thought he was the shit man. This of course I couldn't have you know, someone trying to show me up, making me look like I'm anything but the coolest mother-fucker alive.

He began to move in on my grounds dealing his own shit, and it was shit, to some of the cats I was dealing to. He came in to buy his personal stash from me, not wanting to make it obvious he had his own thing going on, as if I didn't know, as if other people weren't letting me know the straight skinny. His fucking words were so softly spoken, and the smirk on his face was like a knife right into my kidneys, like someone had just kicked my dog in the balls right in front of me and acted like they didn't do it.

I was cool under the guns though, and didn't confront him directly on the matter. I'm sure he knew I knew but the words never came from my mouth. I had something more appropriate in mind for him.

My boy Charlie Federow was infamous for getting things done in a discreet, yet holy fuck what happened kind of way. He must have followed his father's lead. When we were kids his pop wanted a built in swimming pool for the new house he had built. Without the cash for such a thing he was caught up in a little pickle. You know that feeling, the one where you get a thought in your head, a desire unlike any other, when all reason and intellect gets lost and winds up getting you fired out your ass on a Sunday morning while reading Mike Lupica's column in the Daily News, so self satisfying and warm.

Mr. F decided to stick his hand in a snow blower then sue the manufacturer for his ignorance. And he won. And we swam like fish for years in that beautiful new Olympic sized swimming pool for many a summer.

I summoned Charlie to my house for a sit down over some whiskey and blow. I told him my situation and we sat silently for ten minutes while he calmly ran various scenarios through his head regarding an appropriate punishment for dickhead Dan. I was popping from my fucking skin waiting, but I realized that Chuck was the man, the fixer, the best man for the situation I was in, so impatiently I continued to wait, as if standing before the judge for sentencing on my second DWI.

Finally he spoke: "Okay. You say he has a car which he can't live without, one which means the world to him. I will steal an old Buick and smash it into his car. You call me next time he's in your store and I'll handle it from there." He shoved one more line of coke up his nose, gave me a big hug, and left.

Chuck's demeanor was incredibly soothing to my tormented, cloudy mind. I knew then that everything was going to be fine, a rare feeling for me in those days, as my mind was usually filled with paranoia and death.

On a Friday evening Dan came in to tan. We had our usual small talk "what's up for the weekend" kind of shit and I sent into room nine to tan. I placed a call to Charlie. It was a short exchange.

"He's here," I said.

"Ok," he replied, hanging up the phone immediately.

The tanning bed Dan was in had a fifteen minute maximum and he took it all. He came walking out and made his habitual stop in the bathroom, then as he was walking back up to the front of the store a tremendous crash was heard outside. The two of us looked at each other in distinctly different ways; mine a satisfied one while his very troubled. We proceeded outside to see what happened.

Goddamn what a scene! A shit brown boat of a Buick had rammed into the back of his pristine set of wheels, smashing it into the brick wall leaving it looking like an accordion. Man the look on his face and body was priceless. He began to ball like a little kid who was told no regarding whether or not he can have ice cream.

"I'm real sorry Dan. There doesn't seem to be any sign of the driver. I'll go in and call the police."

By this time a crowd of people surrounded his car in awe. I looked around and there, across the street on the other side of the highway at Enzo's Pizza stood Charlie, sucking on a smoke like he just screwed Heidi Klum. With a wink he completed the transaction and went on his way.

Charlie helped many people in this way but always charged a ridiculous amount of cash for his services. Mine were always free though. What an upstanding citizen of the good old United States of America he turned out to become.

The police came and made a report but stated there wasn't much hope in finding out who did it. That's right.

"Dan, do you want me to call a cab for you?" I asked, knowing at that moment he knew I was behind the whole thing. It's funny how I didn't have any more competition from him after that. Back to business as usual, now selling the cocksucker grams for seventy-five dollars and small ones of course.

A new butch named Kelly started coming in and swiftly found out I could hook her up with the goods because well, I told her I could. She was much stranger than Leslie the animal in many ways. She lived with a man and words from her own mouth assured me that she indeed was screwing him. She rode a Harley and her hair was extremely short. She worked out daily and was definitely shooting up some steroids. No tits, she had pectorals. Her walk exuded the fact that she would kick anyone's ass that she needed to.

We became good friends immediately. She loved to snort the coke, and I had the same deal with her as with the other dike: give me money and I will give you nowhere near the amount of coke you should get. And oh yeah, you have valiums do you, I'm going to need a bunch of them.

I delivered her order a few times to her house. Talk about a shady deal holy hell. Her house was on the water and fucking big. When I pulled onto her block in my gold Plymouth Acclaim I felt just a bit out of place as the Mercedes' and other rich folk cars lined the streets and driveways.

I pulled into her driveway, got out, and started heading up to the door when she met me halfway. She started speaking loudly to me saying, "Thanks for coming to take a look at the plumbing Eddie, I really appreciate it."

I saw some of her neighbors glancing over inspecting the whole situation, like a bunch of chicken hawks. When we got inside she explained the need for her bullshit story, saying that her neighbors were extremely nosy and catty. No shit. As if I looked like anything but the junkie drunken drug dealer I was. A six year old Ethiopian could read me like a Bazooka Joe comic. A drug sniffing dog would have collapsed from intoxication at first whiff. Who the fuck was this woman kidding?

Upon entering her house I noticed the overwhelming normalcy of it all. Cozy, yet broken in like an old basement. Humphrey Bogart posters collaged the walls. Her dog was an old Labrador, a black one, who was most contented lying around like he owned the joint, and he did.

Kelly was the only thing that didn't fit in, not your textbook lesbian I thought. Oh well, I gave her the coke and she carved out a huge one for each of us to savor. Man I wished I had gotten the hell out of there right away. This lady could shoot the shit man. She began telling me all of the places she's been and how much she enjoyed riding her motorcycle and unfortunately she went on and on and fucking on.

What about me attract the *ugly* muff divers of the world I'll never know, but apparently it's something. Kelly rambled on about the dude she was living with in a way which would suggest she was straight, but holy fuck there's no possible way she was. In fact she probably was holding more balls between her legs than I was. She's the epitome of butch. Stereotypes are certainly unfair, but they're existence is not by accident. Poster kid for lesbian she was.

After thirty minutes and four more lines I had enough so I told her I needed to leave. As she walked me out the front door her man was pulling into the driveway, and don't you know he planted a thick wet kiss on her mouth as they intersected across the front of the garage. Man the drugs must have really been wearing hard on me because anyone I've told this story to assures me that it's all bullshit and impossible to believe. On my own nut sack I swear 'tis. I said goodbye to the jolly old dike and sped the hell out of there. She did lay some Valium on me though, so she was a queen in her own right as well.

The next morning at the store there was a bit of a horrific scene: both dikes, Leslie and Kelly were waiting in the parking lot for me; Leslie sucking on a minted smoke, and Kelly inspecting her motorcycle like a seasoned mechanic. Neither one spoke a word to the other, and as I entered the store Leslie immediately went to the bathroom while Kelly approached the desk.

As soon as Leslie was out of sight Kelly handed five hundred simolians and told me to be at her place at six o'clock sharp. I asked her if I should bring my toilet snake, which made her laugh a little then I sent her on her way.

Leslie came out of the bathroom passing right by Kelly and I must say I felt like I was in a damn Twilight Zone episode. Leslie's sorry ass began crying as she told me that she was out of cash and needed some blow. It sucked to do it, with I myself being there dozens of times, but I told her I couldn't do shit for her. Man I had a chunk in my pocket but fuck that, rules are rules.

She left and told me she'd be back in an hour. And she was, handing me three hundred. I told her I didn't even want to know the tiniest detail and I shudder to think of the poor bastard who she may have blown to get it, perhaps fucked in the ass with the large cock she kept taped between her legs. I fight off a puke as I write this.

A call to fat man and I was swimming in coke once again. By eleven o'clock that morning I was so charged up I needed to take two Valiums to keep my heart from exploding. As I calmed a bit, just a little bit, for I had still been cranking lines after swallowing the pills, Bernadine Matthews came walking through the door.

I knew she had a crush on me and I figured she was as good as any to become my next hostage. I called her Bernie, and truth be told I think that's the thing that brought her up to the "acceptable" level, otherwise she was really just about non existent to me.

You see, being a maniacal Yankee fan naturally Bernie Williams was one of my favorites. To be able to know someone with the same name let alone it be a girl I could hump, well, you can maybe understand my delight. The Yankees were and are god to me, with Yankee Stadium being my place of worship. I bleed pinstripes man.

I invited Bernie to my house to watch a movie that night and agreed to pick her up at eight o'clock. When I got to her house I rang the bell and her mother answered and invited me in. Bernie was still getting ready so naturally the conversation began between the mother and the older sister who conveniently was waiting in the living room, like a giant vulture, and equally hideous. My how they were talking some shit.

"Why would you want to go out with Bernie?" her mother asked, "she's never had a boyfriend. She won't even know what to do when you're with her."

The vulture chimed in. "Bernie's a pretty awkward girl in case you haven't noticed. She still watches Nickelodeon."

I wanted to grab a fucking iron and beat the shit out of the two of them, then press the blazing thing on their faces and erase their sinister smirks. Out walked Bernie and the two began to laugh at her for what she had on. I must admit she did look like a little kid, jean shorts, sneakers, and what looked like Barbie make-up on, but man she was alright. I almost felt bad for her, but really I felt bad for me, the one who actually agreed to hang out with her. You see, that's the type of person I was, me, me, me, and now cocksuckers!

We said goodbye to mommy dearest and her scum bag sister and headed out. When we got in the car she lunged across the seat and began kissing me like the virgin that she was, sloppy and not so sexy, but it was much welcomed I promise you. We decided to go out for dinner, but just then the fat man called. I was waiting for another batch from the plump little fellow and honestly had written the whole thing off as never going to happen. He was in Belmar, about thirty minutes from my place, so naturally I was in a bit of a dilemma, you know, with the virgin with me and all.

When the man calls, you gotta go. No excuses. I thought for a minute while driving and said this unto the ears of the virgin: Here's the deal Bernie. I'm really not such a nice fellow, and in my twisted ways I've accrued many vices, the biggest of which is an exorbitant taste for cocaine and booze. If you can handle the sketchiest of behavior, the need to speed off in any direction at any moment, and basically only getting some acknowledgement from me after I've had my fill, we'll get along just fine. If not, that's ok, and I will turn around and take you home.

"It's alright Eddie. Keep driving," she said, "It's alright."

And she said it with a smile. I guess I finally kidnapped the right girl. Honesty it seems was not such a bad thing, although I'm sure growing up in the household she did Henry the throat slasher could have gotten in her pants after he took her out on a killing spree without any hesitation. Christ.

We made the thirty minute drive in about eighteen, dodging summer time traffic at the Jersey shore. The fat man was actually already there and parked at the inlet on the right up against a wall. I pulled up next to him, with Bernie coming face to face the white devil, a sight extremely terrifying to probably all but her.

"Hand this cash to him," I instructed, "then grab the sack after he counts the money."

I gave Professor Plump a nod and we each drove off our separate ways. When we went around the corner I pulled over so Bernie could drive while I started getting fucked up again. She looked at me while I was chopping with a rather curious kind of look.

"Forget it Bern, this shit will kill you," I told her.

Two lines straight to the brain and we were on our way to dinner after all. We went to a new steakhouse near the beach called Mickey's. Of course I couldn't eat, but I ordered a steak anyhow, along with a beer and goblet filled with whiskey. Bernie didn't drink at all, a practice I couldn't relate to at all. Drinking, I tried to tell her, opens up your soul to all kind of new experiences, referring to the recently given fact that she had never been laid. She refused, so we finished dinner, I sucking down several more beers with whiskey chasers while Bernie was more than satisfied with a fantastic cut of New York Strip which she devoured, then we headed to my house.

While driving, yes I was driving although she was quite sober, I was trying to imagine what in the hell this sober, non alcoholic, non drug taking individual virgin and I were going to do when we got home, knowing the house would be occupied by around fifteen or so degenerate sons a bitches doing every drug on the planet and then some more from Jupiter. She interrupted my thoughts for a minute.

"Will you have sex with me when we get to your place? I want to get it over with because I've been waiting for 5 years (she was 22 at this time) to lose my virginity."

What do you say to that? I chose to tell her in as sweet a voice I could muster, "Don't worry sweetie, it will be over with quickly."

Looking back I probably should have said something different. But oh well, she was just happy to be getting laid, and who am I to deprive a young lady of that?

She didn't enjoy it at all the first time I must say. When we walked in the door the house was full of smoke, which she was allergic to, so I brought her upstairs and sat with her on my bed for maybe two minutes. I told her to watch the tele while I hung out with the boys for a while. Goddamn who the fuck is actually *allergic* to smoke? Many people don't like it I understand, but Christ are you kidding me?

Back downstairs it was grooving man. James Marshall Hendrix echoed throughout the house. Several chicks made our otherwise chaotic backyard look a bit like heaven, one of whom I was extremely sweet on: Melissa Mendola. She was five foot nine from the ground and proportioned like Jayne Mansfield, with long curly golden brown hair.

After turning some cats onto the space coke I just hooked up with I went outside to give the ladies a taste, with Melissa of course getting the straw first.

"Who's that girl you brought home Eddie?" they all seemed to ask at once.

"Why doesn't she came downstairs and hang out with us?"

"You wouldn't believe me if I spoke the truth about her, so I'm not going to waste your time with the words. Anyhow, how 'bout this coke? It's quite nice no?" I responded.

A bit more small bullshit words went back and forth and I then knew I should probably go upstairs and fuck the virgin, after all, she's been a tremendous captive so far, the least I could do was take away whatever innocence remained in her little world after being in mine for a while, you dig?

When I got upstairs I tried opening the door to my room but it was locked. Oh hell. "Open the door Bernie it's me," I said.

She responded like a kid who was dropped in NYC and left for dead, by throwing her arms around me and squeezing me until I felt my fucking head swell up with a lethal combination of cocaine and blood. Wow she was a little timid.

We wound up going at it for a bit, and by this I mean quite a bit due to the booze and coke cocktail I had running through my body allowing me to have to hold out for quite a while against my wishes. Truth of the matter is I wanted to finish immediately and get the hell back downstairs but it's quite hard under those circumstances as any former or current and whatever the fuck else kind of junk head can attest to. By no means am I special in that regard.

Bernie didn't seem to enjoy it that much, but she was screaming the whole time, like some wanna be porn star trying to make her way after the "acting" career failed. She was quite relieved however, that was obvious, and for the first time I saw her actually smile in a way like she meant it. Good for her I thought. As for me, I needed a smoke with all the fixings immediately, so I kissed her and took off for heaven down the stairway, and it smacked me in the face in that way I love it to.

For the rest of the night I periodically went up and first calmed down the little kid waiting for me in my room and then threw her around a time or two and holy fuck I must have made that trip eight times, the last four of which I actually woke her up because shit, who stays awake around the clock without any kind of stimulants? Progressively, after each time she was becoming more comfortable with herself and man, she made me feel quite nice.

Around ten a.m. most of the vampires had left the house leaving only Tony, his girlfriend, and I which, wasn't much fun. We sat there and cleaned up the debris and basically didn't say much. I went up to get some valiums so we all could get some rest and then we slept.

Three in the afternoon awoke me somehow, and Bernie was chomping at the bit to get home, so I threw on some shorts and we sped off.

The car ride was silent, I mean nothing. I was coming out of my skin and just wanted her to get out of the fucking car so I could get back to bed or get more blow. I would have been fine just to have had her open the door so I could kick her out without having to stop.

I pulled in her driveway and she turned to kiss me and said, "Last night was the best night of my life, Eddie. Thank you."

Wow.

Instead of feeling sorry for her, or perhaps even happy for her I was quick to think that she was the most pathetic human being I'd ever had or would come into contact with. So, I continued to hang out with her in this same way for a couple more months, until finally my brain had a legitimate breakdown, and I began actually having some sort of conscience about the whole thing, and much less than gracefully I told her it was done. I was a real romancer indeed.

Looking back I tell you, I dealt with more than my fair share of lunatics and freaks, all kinds. In a way I was a shrink for these tanners, a bartender and a shrink. I'd hear everything they had, all of it, in great detail, then I, the craziest cat of all gave them advice, and the kicker is most followed it, as if I was the great philosopher of the day overseeing the future and having all the answers all the while feeding seventy percent of them the purest cocaine on the east coast and wondering to myself at night, why do these idiots listen to me? I'll say, I've been in those shoes myself, but fuck, come on fools, I'm going to sell to you whether you listen to me or not, just don't step on my toes or maybe a Buick might come *your* way.

On a cloudy morning I got a call from Leslie the animal butch, and rare from she was in. She was struggling to come up with cash for her daily reprieve from reality, and a more disheartening display of emotion I do not remember encountering before or since.

Now, you know you're your in a pathetic state when I, Lord of disarray, brand you as a hopeless, disgusting, why don't you hang yourself kind of being. I mean hell; countless times a good old fashion noose was exactly what I needed. But Leslie, shit, she was bad.

She told me she needed a large favor, and man did she. She asked me if I could call a American Express and pose as her father, her eighty five year old father, and request a thousand dollar advance on his card because apparently she used it so much they needed direct authorization from her pop in order to make any more funds available. Well shit, I was certainly a thief, a lying cheating absolute scum bag of one, but her request set me back a bit in thought. You see, I needed my daily rake from her bag of goods, so I was in a pickle.

After a moment or two, I decided to make the call, and I'll say once I made up my mind I felt no guilt about it whatsoever. The call itself lasted only a minute, with the card cleared for cash advances. Back in the mid nineties identity theft was not nearly as big a deal as it is now. Thank god.

I dropped a line to the fat bastard, and he assured me a speedy round trip to and fro the magic beautiful super fun time terrific god himself who held the goods. Superb.

Around lunch time fats called me and informed me he didn't have enough time to stop home and separate the ounce of blow into two, not so equal sacks. He did have his scale on him so I told him to come inside the salon when he arrived and we would chop it up in the office.

The chunk of a man never walked into my store before, and when he did I felt my two worlds colliding. Thankfully no customers were inside, not that I wouldn't have left them all to go do the deal if they were, but it was smooth to be able to walk straight back to the chop zone with at least a comfortable ten solid minutes available to hack up my shit.

We got to the office door with sumo man yapping away about the trials and tribulations he had to endure in order to live the way he was living. You know the risks he took, the consequences he faced, all that morning after kind of fox hole shit people like us would think about the day after our shady times the night before. Funny how we wound up doing it all over and over again without any capacity to remember how terrible we felt just a day or a few hours before. Insanity indeed.

I swung the office door open and to my shocking disbelief Sonny the owner was sitting down at the desk having come in from the back door without my knowledge. I nodded in horror to him and more than swiftly went into the bathroom with the large one left holding his dick, paralyzed in fear with no idea whether to walk out or start a conversation.

From inside the toilet I heard him making small talk with Sonny, as if the two of them were in the Vietnam War together. Sonny wasn't having any of it, but in that calm yet frighteningly way he possessed, he was smooth and certainly comfortable in his own skin in not saying anything, I mean *anything,* in response.

After flushing a tremendous shit I was helplessly forced to take I walked out and walked out of the office with captain fats and went back up front, grabbing the ounce of blow from him figuring I'd just cut the gold ball myself. He was sweating a good sweat, I mean when your invisible neck is swallowed by your head you tend to get hot, but this particular kind of sweat was certainly induced mostly from the occurrence not yet two minutes old.

When Sonny came up front roughly forty five minutes later I started explaining the reason why man of the fatness was coming into the office with me but he was hearing none of it, proceeding to walk right by me and out the front door to go see his wife at her hair salon a couple of doors down. I hate that shit. Say something, call me an asshole, knock my lights out, do or say *something* man, I'm having a fucking aneurysm!

Sonny and I never discussed the episode, we didn't need to. He endured my bullshit so long as I kept sales up and customers happy he really didn't make any fuss with me. In fact, many times he and I would drink some beers at the store after we closed, with me of course making several trips to the bathroom to have a snort. More respect for a person I could not have. Unspoken words sometimes speak loudly, especially from one Italian to another.

Many strippers would come in during the daytime, before the noon rush at the tittie bar, to work on their tan lines and maybe score a little toot. Two of the finest were the Formachelli sisters, Laura and Lisa. Lisa, the older of the two, and apparently on the decline regarding her drug use, had long curly blonde occasionally black hair, and a full compliment of tits and ass.

Laura was five years younger and her get up featured a tighter, harder body, but her face was quite weathered as she was still heavily into the scene. It was also not such a secret that she turned a few tricks after work to the "high class rich men" as one of her friends described it. Now, I'm not sure about all that. I can tell you that her pussy would announce her arrival long before her body did, and not with a fishy, fresh salmon. It was like a combination of sour milk and dead dog.

So given this information, like you may in fact feel, I assumed Lisa was the peach of the two, not a saint but sort of a tidy little whore. After all, she had two kids and was driving a nice car, had a respectable looking dude who was the father of *both* of her children.

We had a little trouble at the store for about a week: someone kept taking a shit in one of the garbage cans in the tanning rooms. We were quite busy at that time, as proms were coming up so of course the little teeny boppers needed to look good, so when they got hammered and the dresses flew off after the dance they'd look hot.

Matt, one of the bed cleaners came out the room in disgust and said to me, "What should I do Eddie? There's shit in the garbage again."

"You should clean up the fucking shit and spray down the room you little prick. We got people waiting to tan!" I ordered, like Hitler sending his men to Russia in the winter.

After a few more little "presents" we narrowed it down to Lisa being the culprit, that dirty filthy sack of shit. Having seen her ass up close and in my face before, while checking her out at the club she worked, I felt like I was ripped off you know? That nice, sculpted view from the back of her spread out and ready was tainted now, that little bitch.

I felt like telling anyone who came in the store that she SHIT IN MY FUCKING STORE. I mean what the fuck man; she always went to the bathroom right after she tanned. Why wouldn't she shit in there? What did she do in there? Did she need to brush her teeth because she not only shat in the room but also munched on it? Was she a goddamn log muncher?

I decided not to say much due to the fact that the more I spoke the longer she'd have to be in my sight and I was quite disturbed after the evening's revelation. I did ask her if she knew where the bathrooms were, and in doing so, I'm sure she got my point. From that day on I didn't see one of her little turds again.

Heather, Reagan, Kimberly, Evelyn, Olivia, Tracey, Kimmie, Colleen; more hostages.

Eventually, inevitably, the whole god damn scene became too much to bear. After forcing an inordinate amount of coke up my nose for so long and swallowing enough booze for the lifetime of several good old boys at the local Moose Lodge the shit just wasn't working anymore. I couldn't get high, I couldn't get drunk, I couldn't stay sober. It wasn't fun anymore you dig?

I had a buddy who took Xanax for anxiety. I mean he really had anxiety. He wasn't a junk head like me. He would lay a few on me here and there for a free tan. He came in one day and I asked him if I could buy the whole damn bottle when he got it refilled. He responded in the affirmative, as he never used the whole prescription, ninety a month and he had plenty left to get him through an entire month so giving a hack like me his refill wouldn't hurt him at all. He told me he'd fill his script soon and bring it to me.

It's a hell of a thing waiting for someone to bring you a cocktail for death man. The only good thing in my life at the time was a new young gal I was seeing named Veronica. I remember each day waiting to see if my boy would be coming in at last, looking in the mirror and thinking how much I wanted to stay alive but I couldn't imagine doing it while still living the way I was. An alternative I could did not fathom. Thoughts of Veronica swam around my head. I really liked this girl and I hadn't even screwed her yet.

Four days passed filled with misery and anticipation of peace. Finally my boy came in with the bottle of little coffin nails for me. What relief I felt. What absolute calmness came over me, knowing it would all be over soon, that the feeling of hopelessness would be leaving me that night. I was a sick soul ready for the end.

The rest of the day at work was smooth. Conversing with customers I'd never see again brought me deeper into a state of acceptance. I was in a good spot in my clouded, deranged, unreachable mind, and there was no doubt that the decision I made to die was the correct one. I figured people in my life at that time, friends, family alike, would definitely understand and after a month or so of grief and what not their lives would be much easier without me around to fuck them up. Indeed I was sick, dead inside, just a body without a soul, a host for organs surely pleading for the end as they had been working in vain to endure pure chaotic hell for some ten years.

I stopped in to see Uncle Charlie for my ritual beer and booze run after work, and bought two fake Cubans from him. Funny thing is I actually had to pay for my alcohol, a deed I'd not done for months. Yeah, it was time to move on indeed.

When I arrived at home Tony and I burned a baseball bat sized joint and bullshat over some drinks for about an hour. He informed me he was going to the city, New York that is, to the clubs that night to get his fill of ecstasy and all that accompanied it. I never dug that scene at all, it seemed ridiculous to me, with all the gay type shit that went on there and all. Screw that.

Anyhow, I had a life to kill so the news of the house being vacated for the night fit right in with my plans. I wasn't sending out a cry for help. I didn't want to be talked out of it, in fact I couldn't have been, so a lonely house did make things much easier to carry out with no lifelong friends and otherwise rather close acquaintances around, especially since now no one would be knocking on my door to give or get them some coke.

By this time I was in total isolation. I would come home from work to a crowd of folks and immediately go upstairs and lock myself in my room, even bringing all of my booze upstairs instead of putting the beer in the fridge as I didn't want to have to go downstairs and talk to or see anyone for even a minute. Warm beer suited me just fine.

Tony left the house a few hours later and without hesitation I began my descent into the great unknown. I decided not to leave a note behind due to the fact there was nothing to say. I was a paranoid recluse and didn't feel like explaining to whole fucking thing to anyone. I wanted to die is all.

Up in my room with all things scattered and smoke infested I sat on my bed and thought about the song I wanted to hear before checking out. I decided on Pearl Jam's "All Those Yesterdays". Quite fitting. I put the disc in and set it for repeat.

Ninety Xanax I scattered on the bed beside me, six Heinekens within reach along with a bottle of insulin for the final touch, certainly enough to do the job. By the fistful I swallowed the pills, washing them down with gulps of beer. I drew up the insulin, fifty units at a time and plunged the needle into my stomach. Repeatedly I took shots and after three hundred units I was satisfied my goal would be accomplished as I've never taken more than forty units in any one sitting.

I laid down in absolute peace, right with the world, with my choice, with the certainty of desiring the uncertainty of what lies ahead when my lifeless body transcended into something more or wound up in a box forever staring at darkness being correct. I heard the song one last time and drifted into a comfort level I've ever experienced, quite serene until at last I was gone.

Unfortunately I awoke in a hospital room with ten or so family members and friends hovering over my bed. A tube was hanging from my dick with a respirator pumping oxygen into my body and a couple of bags of fluid swimming in my veins.

Fuck! Man was I pissed. I couldn't even succeed at suicide. The worst part was no one knew what happened figuring it was just another crazy evening for me and the reasons they were there were of course to see me snap out of it but also to have an intervention.

For two days I was in and out of consciousness and the docs were not entirely sure if I was going to make it. Cries from my mother are etched in my mind to this day so clearly. I finally came back to stable and began to get a grasp on just how fucking unfortunate I was to still be alive. My parents and the doctors were speaking about how in fact I pulled through. The docs found extremely high levels of cocaine and Xanax in my system, and my blood sugar level was seventeen upon my arrival.

My friend Tony found me collapsed in my room when he returned from the city around noon on the day of my deed. He called an ambulance and my mother, who, was driving into work at the time and actually had an overwhelming feeling that something was terribly wrong with me. We had that kind of connection my whole life, but hell this time seemed quite crazy.

Apparently after I hit my bed to die I blacked out and placed a call to the fat man. He spotted me an ounce of blow, I guess I figured I'd not have to repay him, and then I called several miscellaneous people, anyone I got a hold of and had them over for a night of indulgence. According to most of them I was in great spirits, smiling and having a genuine good time, fully aware of the events going on. They stayed over until the late morning and when they left they said I seemed to have a certain glow about me, one which they couldn't entirely explain because of its uniqueness.

I snapped up from the hospital bed and to my father I explained what I had done and a look of relief came over his face, like a dope head who's just spiked his vein with sweet goodness. The doctors and my mother returned to my side and I explained to them exactly how I tried to die. After a few minutes one of the doctors told me that he could explain the cocaine counteracting the Xanax but as for the huge amount of insulin I took "There's no medical reason why you're alive right now".

The look on my mother's face still rattles my bones to this day. Wow the pain, the relief, the sorrow, the heartache it encompassed. Selfish to the extreme I was in trying to die man. Had I succeeded everyone close to me would have suffered much more than they had through all of my previous episodes of bullshit. I realize this now much more than I did then.

After two more days I left the hospital and with the suitcase my mother packed for me I made my first of many trips to the nut house. I figured at this point I needed to try to get some help seeing that I couldn't even die and that my time here apparently had been extended for some reason which I couldn't understand. It sucked man, I still wanted to booze it up and ski the slopes of coke but the jig was up. My parents, who at this time were paying all of my bills, were not willing to anymore, at least not if I continued doing the shit that I was.

I said goodbye to my mother and walked alone into the damn rehab/Looney bin, quite unsure of what I got myself into. The nurse who admitted me sent me off with an older woman who had to strip search me for contraband all. This was not a highlight in my life, as I recall her pinching my balls together to see if anything was underneath. As for the anal inspection well, not so pleasant either.

She confiscated the hair gel I made my mother stop and buy for me before arriving because it had alcohol in it. My deodorant: likewise. She told me to get dressed then handed my shoes, minus the shoelaces to me, informing me I was on suicide watch. My anti everything returned and I snapped at her.

"Who the fuck are you lady? I couldn't kill myself with a fucking atomic bomb and you wanna take my shoelaces because you're afraid I could hang myself with them? You're insane, you dirty ole whore!"

A team of looney tune doctors burst in the door to calm me down, forcing a straight-jacket around me and then took me to the isolation room. Fantastic, I thought. This was going to be quite an adventure indeed. Thirty minutes and already I'm the asshole, but it was a comfortable spot for me as I played the asshole role to critical acclaim over the past few years.

The cool thing was the place offered me a break from the tortuous routine I was accustomed to. No drug deals, no paranoia, no booze, and especially no people I knew. There was a brief moment where I was almost willing to conform to the ways of the place and all of it's ideals but it was short lived. I said the right things and took the happy pills they said I needed but as for trying to change my brain well, after two days it was back to screw you I know what's best for me douche bag.

At breakfast one morning I noticed a particularly strange off the wall out to lunch looking mother-fucker. He was eating a bowl of frosted flakes and he was all business man, a machine: spoon to the mouth, eleven chews while holding the spoon ever so still halfway between his mouth and the bowl of delicious goodness on the table. His eyes were fixated on a picture on the wall, one which showed the apparent good life awaiting us all if we put the cork in the jug and our noses clean, with a man evidently returning home from rehab into the loving arms of his family. I couldn't stop studying this man. Nothing seemed to be able to distract him in the slightest.

After he finished I followed him out into the courtyard where everyone else in the place went to smoke and fraternize with each other. You'd be surprised how much *more* you want to screw after being void of toxins for a few days and actually eating three meals a day, my god it was like I was thirteen again when I just discovered what my boys were actually there for you know?

I watched him walk along the path which ran along the circumference of the place. Again he was all business, with no wasted motion. He walked in right angles, those which Joe Pythagoras must have had in his mind while figuring the art of triangles. As he approached his intended destination, a gazebo with a pristine mystique about it, he looked like an alien who commanded an overpowering aura, one which had me entranced like a virgin to her first conqueror.

I kept staring at this cat. After a few minutes he started glanced over at me, on my count every ten seconds. I wouldn't look away, I couldn't. Back and forth he looked my way then back to the beautiful blue jays flying around their nest to his left, my right. It became a competition for me. I wasn't going to stop staring until he made some sort of concession to me, declaring me the victor. My fucking eyes were full of rage, and soon I felt like I was piercing his skull and deteriorating his mind.

Finally he left his post and headed around the circle heading my way. That's right man, you lose. He strolled right up next to me and didn't say a word. I reciprocated the silence and there we stood for several minutes. Hell, I could have stood there forever, with all pills they had me on I felt like jelly, rather jam, so whether an alien or just a strange mother-fucker I wasn't budging.

Finally he spoke. "You know, you and I are the sanest individuals in this place. It's good to know at least one person besides me doesn't belong in here."

I paused for a moment, blown away by the man's statements.

"I don't know man, my sense of sanity went away a long time ago, and after watching you eat breakfast and glide around this sidewalk like a fucking queer finally void of the foot long cock in his ass, I assure you that your brains made their exit from your body long ago in a marble match sometime when you were a kid," I responded.

It was at that moment I realized his situation: he was a rain man, autistic. This was great man. I always wanted one of them in my stable of pawns, my army of freaks and weirdoes ready to be lead in any direction by me, the King of fools himself!

I started hanging out with him every day all day. I dug at his mind to see how his sheer genius could be used for my gain. Following the movie "Rain man" it was quite clear to me that he and I needed to bust out of the joint and head for Atlantic City, just forty five minutes down the Garden State Parkway.

For a genius this cat could certainly be directed like a dog. I told him straight out of my idea and he was all for it. Of course I didn't disclose the "breaking out" part I simply stated we were going on a trip. For three days we hung out and talked. No cards were allowed inside but I knew he could count as many decks as AC dared to implement at their blackjack tables just by speaking to him. All business, that's right.

With one of my two allotted phone calls I called Stephen Fante, a degenerate gambler I've known forever and he agreed to pick us up the following night around midnight. Rain man and I would meet at the water fountain in the hallway and then proceed to simply walk out the goddamn front door with the alarm going off and all then run to Fante's multi shades of blue colored Caprice Classic and be off. Hey, it sounded brilliant to me at the time in its simplicity.

Next night we indeed met at the fountain. I asked rain man if he was ok and he responded in the affirmative. Down the hall past the desk we went until finally reaching the front door exit then we darted outside like two junkies although he wasn't a junkie just a genuine textbook loony who had stopped taking his meds. Myself, well, you know the story by now.

Steve's run down car looked like a giant pussy would to a man just released from solitary for seven years. The alarm was sounding and it wasn't long before six security guards and hospital employees tackled the both of us smashing my goddamn face into the pavement and leaving the rain man utterly helpless and crying on the ground next to me. I heard Steve's car burn the hell out of there along with my hopes of a triumphant black jack run. Damn, I couldn't even get out of the fucking parking lot.

Back inside we went and as it was clear that I was the one who came up this ridiculous scheme the rain man was escorted to his room without any repercussions. For me, well I was to be thrown out the next morning. Motherfucker too, I just got my shoelaces back the previous afternoon.

My dear old mom picked me up with a disgusted look tattooed on her face. I couldn't blame her you know. On the drive home she told me I could stay with her and my father provided I didn't drink, drug, or cause any harm to the family. Wow what a list of demands, at least the drink and drug parts!

I never intentionally caused harm to my family, it's just that by living the way I did, in a fog that is, and all around me were to be affected negatively. I was a tornado sucking up everything along my path. I was blind to this reality though and I wouldn't stop until I had enough pain. Failed suicide didn't wake me up. Shakes from booze and coke couldn't do it. And certainly no chick was going to do it.

Okay mom, I promise you I'm finished with my old life.

And for a week I was but I missed my friends: My wound giving all powerful god-like friends, booze, drugs and drama. You see it's quite difficult for me to let go of something until I am absolutely assured that I can't have at least one more good time with it. I didn't feel like this time would be anything different from all of the previous times, I knew what would happen. I desired it though, the misery and guaranteed hopelessness, with one occasional, and by this I mean rare, good night. I was comfortable being the lost cause in fact I reveled in it. The bad news kid, I loved that shit. That's right feel sorry for me mother-fuckers.

I deserved your sympathy I felt, even wore it like a trophy. The Great One, the genius, the starving artist, I was all of these and when I needed something you had I just took it: Your heart, your money, your kindness and comfort. Essentially everyone on this earth was there to please me, no matter what I did to them, however terrible and crude I was. Fuck you, it's about me man.

Anyhow, quick suicide obviously wasn't in the cards for me, so I decided to drink myself to death, a process filled with great suffering and slow torture carried out over endless monotony, in other words, one long day of shit stretched out indefinitely.

My job at the Tropicalia lay in wait, but it was imperative that I left town immediately and without anyone being the wiser. I packed up a small sack of clothes along with enough cocaine and booze to get me where I needed to be, which wasn't exactly determined in my mind. I figured I'd head south from Jersey and see what happened.

So here I sit folks, in a ramshackle quiet little town in North Carolina. In my present state of mind this is all I am certain of. I've been here a couple of years and as I write this I'm enjoying a tall glass of six dollar a bottle whiskey in a run down holy fuck this is what I've become little bar. I'm not happy but most content.

A super terrific fantastic grocery store allows me to work third shift stocking shelves. I can drink on the job and take full advantage of it. My bills, three hundred a month for rent in a luxurious little one room apartment which suits me just fine, along with fifty a week for food are paid for. That leaves me with around one hundred fifty for booze a week, a meager amount but enough to keep me twisted most of the time.

Next door to me lives an older gal named Valerie who kindly allows me to get on top of her once and again and she's actually pretty damn cute. I've gone out trolling for cocaine several times but only made one connection and the shit he had was bottom of the barrel at best, thus my coke days seem to have subsided for now.

Valerie bought a little lap top for me and though the transition from paper and pen to typing has been difficult it was necessary. She's convinced of my talents and tells me that my work, mainly poetry and short stories, are nothing short of spectacular, and I believe her. She has a way of making me feel like I'm the most important person in the world, which leaves me feeling guilty each time I stray.

Natalie, Theresa, Lisa, Laura, and Darcy.

www.ingramcontent.com/pod-product-compliance
Lightning Source LLC
Chambersburg PA
CBHW051803040426
42446CB00007B/491